THE
VOLUNTEER
AND
INTELLIGENT SOLDIER's
COMPANION.

Containing Inſtructions for Officers and Privates, the form of a Review, manner of performing
THE EIGHTEEN MANOEUVRES,
The Manual and Platoon Exerciſes, as ordered for the Infantry of
HIS BRITANNIC MAJESTY;
With other Military Information, illuſtrated by Notes, and Embelliſhed with
THIRTY COPPERPLATES.

" And this know, that if the good man of the houſe had known what hour the THIEF would come, he would have watched, and not have ſuffered his houſe to be broken through:—— BE YE THEREFORE READY."
LUKE XII. 39,40.

The Naval & Military Press Ltd

published in association with

FIREPOWER
The Royal Artillery Museum
Woolwich

Published by
The Naval & Military Press Ltd
Unit 10 Ridgewood Industrial Park,
Uckfield, East Sussex,
TN22 5QE England
Tel: +44 (0) 1825 749494
Fax: +44 (0) 1825 765701
www.naval-military-press.com

in association with

**FIREPOWER
The Royal Artillery Museum, Woolwich**
www.firepower.org.uk

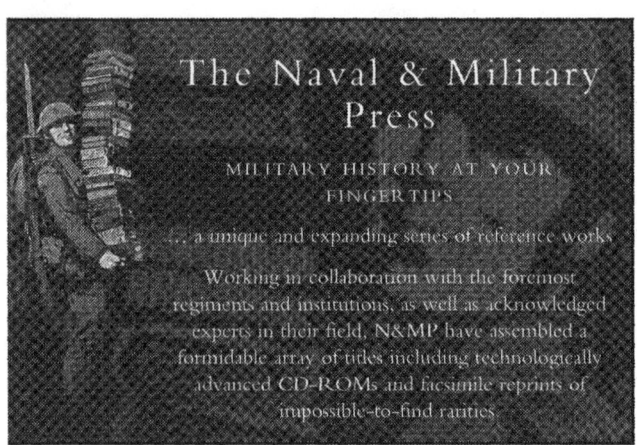

In reprinting in facsimile from the original, any imperfections are inevitably reproduced and the quality may fall short of modern type and cartographic standards.

ADVERTISEMENT.

The following sheets lay no claim to originality, and for all the errors the Editor is alone accountable.

Hints of improvement, with corrections will be thankfully received, and carefully attended to, should a second impression ever be called for, and whatever additions may then be made, will be given gratis to the purchasers of this edition.

Elliot's Rooms.
August 16. 1803.

REGIMENTAL UNIFORM

OF THE

FIRST REGIMENT OF ROYAL EDINBURGH VOLUNTEERS.

(See the Frontispiece.)

A LONG Coat of the best Scarlet Cloth, with blue facings pointed at the top, three pair Button-holes, and one at the top wrought with twist. The upper hole to be $2\frac{1}{4}$ inches from the top of the facing. Breadth of the facing at the top hole 5 inces, at the under one 3 inches. The length of the facing to be in proportion to the man, so as to shew two inches of the vest. The coat to hook down the breast, with one hook at each button-hole

A Blue Cape, with a scarlet front, the front $4\frac{1}{2}$ inches long, with a button and hole wrought with twist.

A Dragoon-Sleve and cuff, with two pair of button holes wrought with twist. The distance from the bottom of the cuff to the centre of the upper hole to $7\frac{1}{2}$-inches.

The Facings, Cape, and Cuff to be edged with white.

Ring-

Ring-wings gilt, made up on scarlet, with a narrow gold binding, and edged with blue.

Peaked pocket flaps, with two pair button-holes wrought with twist. The back of the coat with one pair of wrought button-holes.

The Skirts of the coat turned up with white kerseymere, running and widening from the bottom of the facing to within about 3 inches of the bottom of the skirt, where the facings meet, and are joined with a metal ornament edged with blue. The Grenadiers with a metal grenade.

The coat to reach exactly to within two inches of the bend of the hough,—to be short in the waist,—lined with white shalloon, and faced up the inside of the breast with kerseymere.

The Vest and Breeches of white kerseymere.—The Vest single breasted.—The breeches with four buttons at the knee, with a regimental plain yellow buckle.

Long Gaiters of Black cloth, with small regimental button,

A black velvet Stock, tied before with black ribbon, but concealed.

The pattern coat, &c. to be seen at Conveener Ranken's, Parliament square. And notwithstanding these directions, it is requested that it be attentively examined; for the Uniform of every Volunteer will be inspected by an officer, and if not according to the Pattern, will be thrown upon the maker's hands.

A Regimental Hat is preparing, which will be
shewn

shewn in a few days at George Hunter's, army clothier, South Bridge Street.

Round Hat, full Inch Yeoman Crown: Depth, seven Inches, turned close up at the side:—To be mounted with Gilt Star plate, having Thistle in the Centre, and full Military Composition Cockade, with Centre Star of Ditto, upon which is placed a Regimental Button:—To have a Regulation Feather $12\frac{1}{2}$ Inches long in front.

The Grenadier Hat to be One Half Inch higher than the Battalion,—to have a White Feather the same Length, and a small Grenade in place of the Button in the Centre of the Rose;—these to be the only distinction between the Battalion and Grenadiers.

TO THE

RIGHT HONOURABLE

CHARLES HOPE,

LORD ADVOCATE OF SCOTLAND, MEMBER OF PARLIAMENT FOR THE CITY OF EDINBURGH,

and

LIEUTENANT-COLONEL OF THE FIRST REGIMENT OF ROYAL EDINBURGH VOLUNTEERS.

MY LORD,

SHOULD the following designs, exhibiting the various Evolutions of a Regiment of Infantry, and the Instructions with which they are accompanied, be the means of assisting my Brethren in arms, in forming correct Ideas of the Soldier's Duty, the purpose of their publication will be completely answered.

At the same time, it affords an opportunity of expressing not only my own, but the sentiments of a whole Battalion—that your Lordship may long fill the many important offices of trust committed to your charge, and continue to command a corps, which owes its very existence, and any steadiness of which it may boast, entirely to your persevering exertions.

In these times of alarm, may every Briton, animated by your Soldierlike example, with firmness and alacrity, hasten to the unfurled standard of his native country.

I have the honour to be,

My LORD,

Your Lordship's Humble Servant,

A Private, R. E. V. Reg. 1st.

CONTENTS.

	Page
Hints to the Officer	1
——— *to the Soldier*	2
Formation of a Company	3
——————— *of a Battalion*	6
Detail of a Regiment	7
Battalion in close order	10
Manner of telling off the Battalion	11
Firings	13
Formation of Guards	22
Forms of sending for and lodging the colours	29
——— *of a Review*	32
Manual exercise	42
Platoon exercise	49
Eighteen Manœuvres	57
Military Funerals	130
Feu de joie	134

THE
VOLUNTEER
AND
INTELLIGENT FOOT SOLDIER'S
COMPANION.

We shall suppose the officers and soldiers of a regiment of infantry able to go through the *manual* and *platoon exercises* with steadiness and accuracy; and to have acquired a perfect knowledge of the various *marchings, wheelings, dressings, steps, formings* &c. in single rank company and battalion; in short completely drilled; they are now in uniform, and about to be inspected by a general officer, prepatatory to immediate service.

THE OFFICER

Besides being completely master of every part of the private's duty must have learned the sword exercise and words of command, which last should always be given, even to the smallest bodies, in the full extent of the voice, and in a sharp tone. It is not sufficient that he is heard only by the platoon under his immediate command, the leaders of others who are dependent on his motions muſt hear alſo.

Every officer muſt alſo acquire the habit of readily aſcertaining by the eye, the perpendiculars of march, and the ſquareneſs of the wheel; he muſt not only know the poſt he ſhould occupy in all changes of ſituation, but the intention and uſe of every movement, the principles on which it is made, and the faults that may be committed, in order to avoid them himſelf, and to inſtruct others.—Theſe principles are in themſelves ſo ſimple, that moderate reflection and attention, will ſoon ſhew them to the eye, and fix them in the mind.

An officer who cannot thoroughly diſcipline and exerciſe the body intruſted to his command, is not fit in time of ſervice to lead it to the enemy; he cannot be cool and collected in the time of danger ; he cannot profit of circumſtances, from an inability to direct others ; the fate of many depends on his ill or well acquitting himſelf of this duty.—It is not ſufficient to advance with bravery ; it is requiſite to have that degree of intelligence, which ſhould diſtinguiſh every officer according to his ſtation ; nor will ſoldiers ever act with ſpirit and animation, when they have no reliance on the capacity of thoſe who conduct them.

THE SOLDIER

In the midſt of ſurrounding noiſe and confuſion, muſt have his eye and ear attentive *only* to his own immediate officer, with whoſe voice he ſhould early become familiar, and the loudneſs of whoſe commands

inſtead

instead of creating unsteadiness, should reconcile him to the hurry inseparable from action.

FORMATION OF A COMPANY

Every company is formed three deep, and sized from flanks to centre, and a size roll kept for this purpose; the tallest is in front, the next tallest in the rear, and the shortest in the centre, which formation may be thus performed: Place the shortest man in the centre, the next tallest on his left, the next tallest on his right, and so on alternately till the tallest of all are on the flanks; tell off the rank in six divisions, the right and left divisions are to compose the *front rank*, the two divisions from the right and left nearer the centre, are to compose the *rear rank*, and the two divisions in the centre, the *centre rank*.

FORM RANKS, *or three deep form.—March—Halt.*

At the word March, the two divisions on the flanks and the two centre divisions, all step off together, the flank divisions 12 paces, and the centre divisions 6; then, INWARDS *Face—*QUICK *march.—Halt—front.*

There are other methods of forming three deep, but this is preferred *.

The

---

* *This arrangement however, is more for show than real use; the French infantry when preparing for action, make in an instant, intervals in the centre and rear ranks, through which the front rank passes, and they stand thus: The tallest men in the rear, the next tallest in the centre, and the shortest in the front.*

(4)

The company now formed in close order which is the primary and chief order in which the battalion and its parts at all times assemble, the centre closed up one pace from the front, and the rear one pace from * the centre, files lightly touch but no crouding.

The captain is on the right, the ensign on the left of the front rank, each covered by a serjeant; the lieutenant is in the rear behind the right, the drummers behind the left, and the pioneers behind the centre of the fourth or supernumerary rank, three paces from the rear rank †.

Each

The 1st Regiment of Royal Edinburgh Volunteers when last embodied, formed only two deep, but as they were called upon then, for a very different purpose from that for which they now assemble, and their number being more than 1000 rank and file, they should form three deep, the order for which all their operations and movements are calculated.

The formation in two ranks may be regarded as an occasional exception, where an extended or covered front is to be occupied, or where an irregular enemy who deals only in fire is to be opposed, or for light troops in the attack and pursuit of a timid and disorderly mob.

No general could manage a considerable army if extended in this manner, nor could it have any prospect of resisting a determined charge of cavalry, therefore in no service is the third rank to be given up, without it, the battalion would soon be a single rank

* *Open order is occasionally used for parade, inspection of arms, accoutrements, &c. the officers are then advanced three paces in front, the ground equally divided amongst them, and the ranks two paces distant from each other; a serjeant is on each flank of the front rank, the pioneer behind the centre of the rear rank, the drummer on the right of the right serjeant.*

† *The use of the fourth rank is to keep the others closed up during an attack; too many officers and non-commissioned officers cannot be employed on this very important service.*

Each company is generally a platoon, and told off in two divisions and four sections, and when in open column of sections, the captain is on the pivot flank of the leading section, his covering serjeants on the pivot of the second, the ensign on the pivot flank of the third section, and the lieutenant on the pivot flank of the fourth or rear section. The officer who commands the company gives the word for all the sections at once to wheel into line.—*Halt—Dress*.

When the company stands in open column of subdivisions, the commander is on the pivot flank of the leading subdivision, the next in command on the pivot of the next subdivision, the other officer, drummer and pioneer are in the rear of the subdivisions behind which they are placed when the company is in line, the left of the front rank, and the right of the left subdivision should be marked by a corporal, and the places of absent officers with serjeants, corporals, or intelligent privates.

When the open column wheels to the left into line, the covering serjeant is on the right of the division, but when wheeling to the right into line, he goes behind the pivot file.

When the company is to join others, and the battalion or part of it to be formed, the ensign and his covering serjeant quit the rank and fall into the fourth rank, till otherwise posted.

Formation of the Battalion.

The Battalion is 10 Companies,
- 1 grenadier
- 8 battalion
- 1 light infantry

Each Company consists of
- 3 officers
- 3 serjeants
- 3 corporals
- 2 drummers
- 60 privates.

The grenadier and light infantry * companies are also called flank companies. They have each 2 lieutenants, but no ensign—they have also each an extra drummer.

Detail

---

* *The 1st regiment of R. E. V. has no light infantry. The two flank companies are grenadiers.*

DETAIL OF THE REGIMENT.

Field Officers { All captains of companies, viz. }
- 1 colonel
- 1 lieutenant-colonel
- 1 major
- 7 captains
- 12 lieutenants
- 8 ensigns

Staff Officers, { All mustered in the colonel's company, as well as the staff serjeants and drum-major. }
- 1 adjutant
- 1 pay-master
- 1 quarter-master
- 1 surgeon
- 1 mate

Non-Commissioned Officers, { Including the two staff serjeants, viz. the serjeant-major, and quarter-master serjeant. }
- 30 serjeants
- 30 corporals

{ Including drum-major. }
- 22 drummers
- 600 privates

A man from each company, with a corporal to command them, are selected for pioneers; they are under the direction of the quarter-master.

The field officers and the adjutant are mounted.

Flank officers are to wear wings and not epaulets; however the grenadier officers in most regiments wear two epaulets.

The field officers are ordered by the regulation to wear 2 epaulets each.

The colours are carried by the 2 youngest ensigns in most regiments.

When the companies join, and the regiment is formed, there is to be no interval between any of them.

The companies will draw up as follows, from right to left. Grenadiers, 1st captain and major; 4th and 5th captain; 3d and 6th captain; 2d captain and lieutenant colonel; light company *. The colonel's company takes place according to the rank of its captain.

The four eldest captains are on the right of grand-divisions. Officers commanding companies or platoons, are all on the right of the front rank of their respective ones. The regiment will be divided into 2 wings,

* *In militia regiments, where the captain-lieutenant is always junior to every captain of a company, the colonel's company is the right or left centre company.*

wings, right and left wing; four grand-divisions, eight companies or platoons, sixteen sub-divisions, and thirty two sections, when the companies are very strong each company will be divided into two platoons.

When the 10 companies are with the battalion, they may then, for the purposes of firing or deploying, be divided into five grand-divisions from right to left.

The battalion companies will be numbered from the right to the left, 1, 2, 3, 4, 5, 6, 7, 8.—The sub-divisions will be numbered 1, 2, of each;—the sections will be numbered 1, 2, 3, 4, of each; the files of companies will also be numbered 1, 2, 3, 4, &c. The grenadier and light companies will be numbered separately in the same manner, and with the addition of those distinctions.

These several appellations will be preserved, whether faced to front or rear.

The companies must be equalized in point of numbers, at all times when the battalion is formed for field movement.

The commanding officer is the only officer advanced in front, for the general purpose of exercise when the battalion is single; in the march in line, and in the *firings*, he is in the rear of the colours.

One officer is on the right of the front rank of each company or platoon, and one on the left of the battalion.

In general, officers remain posted with their proper companies, but commanding officers will occasionally make such changes as they may find necessary.

Battalion of ten Companies, with two guns on each flank, in close order.

See Plate 1st.

RANKS are at the distance of one pace, supernumerary rank 3 paces from the rear rank, major and adjutant 6 paces in the rear of the 3d and 6th companies

Lieutenant colonel 6 paces behind the rear, in line with the major and adjutant.

Pioneers 2 deep, 9 paces behind the rear rank.

Drummers 6 paces behind the rear rank of the 2d and 7th companies, grenadier and light infantry drummers 6 paces behind their respective companies.

The music 3 paces behind the pioneers—staff, 3 paces behind the music.

When the line is halted, and especially during the firings when engaged, the covering serjeants fall back into the fourth or supernumerary rank.

The colours are placed in the front rank between the 4th and 5th battalion companies, each covered by

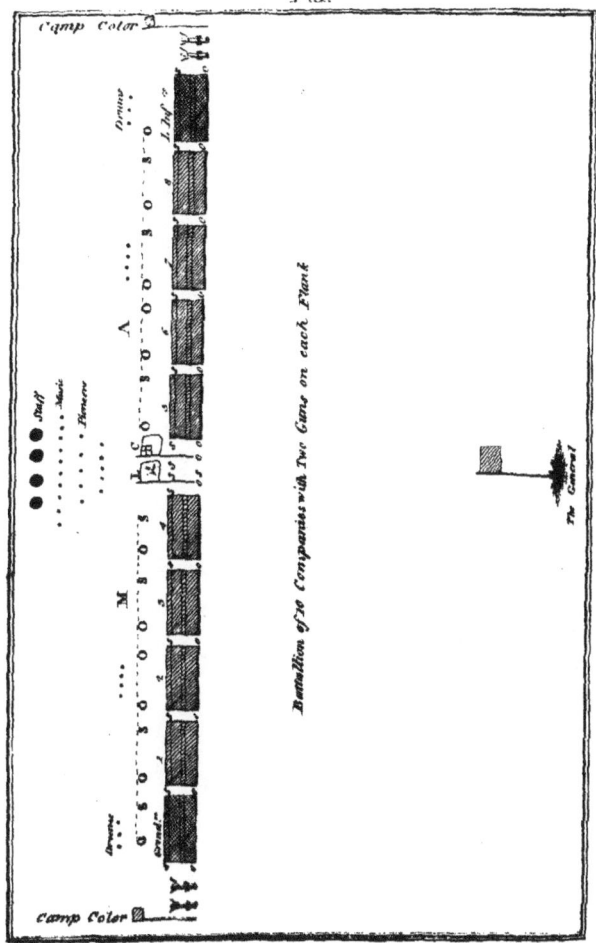

Pl.I.

Battalion of 10 Companies with Two Guns on each Flank

a non-commissioned officer; one directing serjeant is in the front rank betwixt the colours, he is covered by a second in the rear rank, and by a third in the supernumerary rank: The sole business of these 3 serjeants is, when the battalion moves in line, to advance and direct the march.

The march of the battalion in LINE, either to front or rear, being the *most important* and most difficult of all movements, every attention of officers and men become peculiarly necessary.

To attain this end, directing serjeants must be well trained to this peculiar object, on whose exactness of cadence, step, squareness of body, and precision of movement, dependence can be had.

MANNER OF TELLING OFF THE BATTALION.

THE colours are placed in the centre of the battalion, and mark the two wings.

Of the officers appointed to carry the colours, the eldest carries the king's, the youngest the regimental colour.

Whenever the right wing advances or retires, the king's colour accompanies it on its flank, to it the mens eyes are directed as their point of dressing.

In the same manner the regimental colour accompanies the left wing.

The company on the right of the colours. is called the right centre company. the company on the left of the colours, is called the left centre company.

The

The companies from right to left are told off into right and left companies thus, the grenadiers; 2d, 4th, 6th, 8th, are called *right companies*; and the 1st, 3d, 5th, 7th, light infantry, † are called *left* or *alternate companies*:—each company is divided into right and left sections, there shall be 4 file at least in a section; if however the company is not strong enough to have four sections, it should be divided into three sections, each of which ought to have *five file*.

Words of command to be used in trying the battalion.

Right companies,	{ order—*arms* shoulder—*arms*
Left companies,	{ order—*arms* shoulder *arms*
Right sections, Left sections the same,	{ order—*arms* shoulder—*arms*
Right hand men of grand division, Left hand men of &c.	{ order—*arms* shoulder—*arms*
Right-hand men of companies, Left hand men of &c.	{ order—*arms* shoulder—*arms*
Right hand men of sub-divisions and sections, Left hand men of &c.	{ order—*arms* shoulder—*arms*

First

---

† *Or as in the First Regiment of Royal Edinburgh Volunteers, left grenadiers.*

First grand-division,
Second grand-division,   } order—*arms*
Third grand division,   } shou der—*arms*
Fourth grand-division,

Right wing,   } order – *arms*
Left wing the same,   } shoulder—*arms*

The officers should also answer to their numbers, for the opening of the column, and for all their different firings.

Too much attention cannot be given in telling the battalion off correctly.

FIRING.

Sometimes the wings fire independently of each other by sub divisions or companies, as if each wing was a separate battalion.

In firing by sub-divisions, when one fires, the next *presents*—when one *presents*, the next is *ready*, keeping up an incessant fire.

The pause betwixt each of the firing words, *make ready, present, fire*, is the same as the ordinary time, viz. the 75th part of a minute, and no other pause is to be made betwixt the words.

In firing by *grand divisions*, three pauses will be made betwixt the *fire* of each division, and the *make ready* of the succeeding one.

In platoon firing, two pauses will be made.

In firing by wings, one wing will make ready the instant the other is shouldering.

B

In firing companies by *files*, each company fires independent, when the right files present, the next make ready, and so on.—After the first fire, each man as he loads, comes to a recover, and the file again fires without waiting for any other: the rear rank men are to have their eyes on their front rank men, and be guided by, and present with them.

The advance of the battalion should instantly succeed the forming of the line; and when it arrives and halts at the point where it is to fire, the firing ought *instantly* to commence at the word *halt*; for, the battalion having been apprized *during the march*, of the nature of the required firing, no improper delay need therefore be made.

The line, if retiring, *halts, fronts*, at one command, and instantly begins firing, from the centre, and not from the flanks. In other cases, and in successive formations, it may begin from whatever division first arrives, and halts on its ground.

Firing in Line.

Objects of Fire.

1. THE chief object of the fire against cavalry is to keep them at a distance, and to deter them from the attack; as their movements are rapid, a reserve is always kept up. But when fire commences against infantry, it cannot, consistent with order, and other cir-

circumstanses, be too heavy or too quick while it lasts, and till the enemy is beaten or repulsed.

2. The fire of 3 ranks standing is hardly, with our present arms, to be required, especially if the ground should be broken, and that the soldiers are loaded with their knapsacks.

Defensive Fire.

3. Where infantry are posted on heights that are to be defended by the fire of musquetry, the front rank will kneel, that one third of the fire that may be given should not be lost, for otherwise the rear rank in such situation could not sufficiently incline their pieces to raise the slope. As soldiers generally present too high, and as fire is of the greatest consequence to troops that are on the defensive, and who are posted if possible on commanding grounds, the habitual mode of firing should therefore be rather at a low level than a high one, and the fire of the front rank kneeling, being the most efficacious as being the most raising, should not be dispensed with when it can be safely and usefully employed.

In line advancing.

4. When infantry marches in line to attack an enemy, and in advancing makes use of its fire; it is perhaps better to fire the 2 first ranks only standing, reserving the third, than to make the front rank kneel
and

and to fire the whole; but volleys fired at a considerable distance, or on a retiring enemy, may be given by the three ranks, the front one kneeling.

Platoon Firing.

5. A line posted, or arriving at a fixed situation, will fire by *platoons*, each battalion independent, and such firing generally commencing from the centre of each. The first fire of each battalion will be regular, and establish intervals; but after the *first fire* each platoon shall continue to fire as soon as it is loaded, independent and as quick as it can, till the battalion or line is ordered to cease.

File Firing.

6. Behind a parapet, hedge, or abbatis, the two first ranks only can fire, and such fire may be *file firing*, deliberate and cool, the 2 men of the same file always firing together: it may begin from the right or left of platoons, and should be taught in situations adapted to it, not in open ground.—Should the parapet, hedge, or abbatis, be but little raised, platoon firing may be used.

Oblique Firing.

7. *Oblique firing* by battalions is advantageous on many occasions, as when it is proper, or that time

does

does not allow to give an oblique direction to part of a line, or that their fire can in this manner be thrown against the opening of a defile, the flanks of a column, or against cavalry or infantry that direct their attack on some particular battalion or portion of the line.

Regularity of Firing.

8. As long as the fire by battalion, half battalion, or companies, can be kept up regular, it is highly advantageous and can be at any time stopped; but, should file-firing be allowed, and once begun, unless troops are exceeding cool and well disciplined, it will be difficult to make it finish, and to make them advance in order.

When a line halts at its points of firing, no time is to be lost in scrupulous dressing, and the fire is instantly to commence —But a line that halts and is not to fire, or when its firing ceases after the halt, may immediately be ordered to dress from colours to colours.

Street Firing

Is so called from being obliged to engage in a street, highway, lane, or narrow passage, where no more than 10, 12, 16, or 20 files can march in front; so that according to the breadth of the place, the platoons must be stronger or weaker.

When the column is in motion, and arrived where the firing is to begin, the commanding officer *from the*

the rear, gives the word halt, the officer commanding the platoon, inſtantly gives the words *ready, preſent, fire—recover arms, outwards, face, quick march.*

At the word *recover arms*, the platoon immediately in the rear of the one that has fired recover their arms alſo, and cock, and when their front is open by the march of the others down their flanks, they march on with recovered arms until they receive from their officer the words *halt, preſent, fire*, and ſo on.

As ſoon as the platoon has got down the flanks, it muſt form inſtantly in the rear, and immediately prime and load *without halting*, keeping always their exact diſtance from the diviſion before them, which would not be the caſe if they halted to load and ſhoulder.

When this is to be put in practice on real ſervice, the front of the platoons muſt not be equal to the breadth of the place it is to engage in ; but there muſt be a ſmall ſpace of ground or interval left on the flanks, that thoſe who have fired may have room to march back and form in the rear.

It is in this manner, when there is not time to raiſe a breaſt-work, that a paſs, bridge road, or ſtreet, is to be maintained againſt the enemy, by the platoons ſuſtaining one another; and firing in their turn; which may be continued as long as there is occaſion, almoſt without intermiſſion by one battalion only.

In firing as above deſcribed, the colours, &c. muſt at the firſt be placed in the rear, and kept there by the ſub-diviſions as they come down the flanks after

firing

firing, forming conſtantly *in their front*, till the whole buſineſs is over.

There are however different methods of retiring the platoons from the front to the rear.

Some are inſtructed after the word fire, to recover arms, and wheel out the platoon by ſub-diviſion from right to left, load, and remain in that poſition till the laſt platoon paſſes them, when they wheel back and form.

Another method, ſuppoſing the ſtreet to be filled by the platoon, and no room left on the flanks—then by throwing back or retiring a centre ſection of each platoon, the retiring platoon may paſs through the centre of the column to the rear; it looks well in a drawing, and has a good effect on a day of parade, but it is too complicated to be attempted with ſafety in the face of an enemy *.

General obſervations.

There is no doubt but that the fire of the muſquetry may be reduced to a theory: but far from that being the caſe, the ſoldier has no principle given him, for let the diſtance or ſituation of the objects be what they may, he fires at random. It is principally owing to the exerciſe of the target being ſo little practiſed, that this ignorance and deficiency of principle is ſo ſeverely felt.

* *Plate 3d. gives a view of the firings, by Grand-diviſions, Companies, and Sub-diviſions.*

In our firings the foldier is inftructed always to fire low, yet no reafon is given him why it fhould be fo, but that the ball rifes. To confider this a moment:— The line of level * and the line of fire † are by no means parallel, for according to the different weights of metal which the barrel has at its breaching ‡, and at its aperture, fo they defcribe an angle more or lefs acute beyond the tube. As the eye feeks its aim from the length of the line of level, it is therefore fixed at the *exterior* of the barrel. But entirely different to this principle, the motional body, the bullet, is impelled from the *interior* part of the inftrument, and the length of the line of fire, therefore the line of level and the line of fire cut each other. From the law of attraction impofed on all bodies obliquely thrown, at its delivery from the mouth of the cylinder, the bullet or ball defcribes a curve, it cuts the line of level at a fmall diftance from the mouth of the barrel: it will at about the diftance of 60 toifes, or 360 feet be found to be at a foot and a half, or two feet, its greateft elevation above the line of level. From thence drawn to the earth by gravitation, to which all bodies are fubjected, it again inclines to the former line, and at the diftance of about 120 toifes, cuts it a fecond time; it is this fecond point

of

---

* LINE OF LEVEL, *is the ftraight line, by which is feen the object on which the ball fhould be carried to.*

† LINE OF FIRE, *a ftraight line which reprefents the axis of the mufket*

‡ *To remedy this uncertainty, the Germans who are fo famous for their point blank fhots, have their riffle barrels of the fame weight of metal, the whole length of the tube*

of interſection, which is called the muſket ſhot, or *point blank*, after which the bullet finiſhes to deſcribe its *parabola* to the end of its fall. What is here ſaid, is a common property to all fire arms.

It follows, that to make the ball arrive at the mark intended, the ſight muſt not be always preciſely levelled at that mark. Suppoſe a mark ſix feet high divided into three equal parts—if you ſtand at the diſtance of 50 or 60 toiſes, or 360 feet, and mean to ſtrike the upper dimenſion, you muſt take aim at the middle one two feet under the mark; if you mean to ſtrike the middle, you muſt take aim at the lower dimenſion, &c.

If you ſtand at 100 toiſes, the aim muſt be taken one foot below the mark, in order to hit it.

If the diſtance is more than 100 toiſes, to ſtrike any of the dimenſions, aim muſt be taken *above* the mark, and ſo keep raiſing in proportion to the diſtance.

Suppoſe a battalion of the enemy in front, if at 300 toiſes diſtance, aim ſhould be taken three feet over the battalion.

If at 200 toiſes diſtance, about a foot and a half.

If at 150, aim ſhould be taken at their hats.

If at 100, the middle of the body, &c.

Although the horizontal ſhot of a muſket may be computed at 180 toiſes, yet where the fire of a line of infantry can have effect, it is ſeldom more than at 80 toiſes, or 160 yeards *.

See Guibert, v. i. p. 147.

To facilitate the loading quick, BLAND recommends the cartridges to be made up with such exactness, that after they are placed in the muzzle, one thump with the but-end on the ground will make them run down to the breech of the barrel, which he observes will save the time *usually taken up in ramming*. He goes on to say, " but as the ramming down of the cartridge is, in my opinion, very necessary, I must beg leave to offer some objections against the disusing it." After giving many reasons to prefer using the ramrod,—he says, " For these reasons when the men are not *pressed too close* by the enemy, the ramming down of the cartridge should not be omitted on service."

It appears probable, therefore, that 50 years ago, the soldier seldom drew his ramrod in battle; it is evident that it was not, as is now the case, thought to be indispensible.

Many German regiments have their ramrods equally thick at both ends, which prevents the necessity of turning them, and being consequently heavier than ours, one ram down is sufficient.

FORMATION OF GUARDS IN CAMP AND GARRISON.

THERE are three daily beats in camp by the drummers, viz.—The reveillié at day break, when the morning-gun is fired, the troop at guard mounting, and the retreat at sun-set, when the evening-gun is fired

fired. In garrifon the tattoo is beat at 8 or 9 at night, for the foldiers to retire to their quarters.

At reveillé beating, the fentries ceafe challenging, and out-lying picquets or nightly detachments return to camp. The reveillé is beat by the drummers of the quarter-guards, who likewife regulate the other beats. The drummer on the quarter guard on the right, beats two taps on the drum a quarter of an hour before the time appointed for guard-mounting, and about the fame time at fun-fet; the drummers of all the other quarter guards from right to left repeat the fame, and as foon as it has reached the guard on the left of all, the drummer of it returns it back again to the right. The firft drummer then beats the drummer's call, which likewife goes from right to left, and back again.

If the guards are ordered to mount at nine o'clock, the drum-major of the regiment on the right, orders his drummers to beat off at that hour, the other drum-majors taking the fignal from him.

The fame is obferved at fun-fet in beating the retreat, previous to picquet mounting, and evening roll-call.

The manner of mounting and relieving the quarter guard in camp, will fuffice as a general direction for mounting and relieving all guards in camp or garrifon.

As foon as the taps are given by the drummers of the quarter-guards, the men for guard affemble in
their

their ſtreets, where the orderly corporals examine them, to ſee that the men are clean, their arms and their accoutrements in good order.

During the beating of the troop, the orderly corporals march the men up to the ſerjeant's ſtreet, facing the parade. On the finiſhing of the troop, the adjutant on the right of the line, gives the word of command, *advance to form the guard, march:* all the other adjutants from right to left do the ſame. The men with carried arms, and non-commiſſioned officers with recovered arms, both thoſe for guard as well as orderly, march forward in quick time to the line of parade; which having reached, they are again ordered to *form the guard;* on this they face inwards, and as they come oppoſite to the colours of their regiment, the centre files mark time till thoſe on the right and left come up to them; they are then *halted, fronted, and dreſſed* in a rank intire. The non-commiſſioned officers for guard, ſix paces in front, and the orderly corporals eight paces from them, facing the guard.

The adjutant examines the men's arms, accoutrements and dreſs; if any thing is amiſs, the orderly corporals are anſwerable for it. Two men are generally turned out to act as orderlies to the commanding officer and the adjutant of the regiment; for that purpoſe the cleaneſt ſoldiers are made choice of.

The adjutant gives the word of command, *ſerjeant and corporals, recover arms, right and left face, quick march;* thoſe for guard take poſt, and the orderly corporals go to their companies.

The

The guard receives the following words of command from the adjutant, *order arms, fix bayonets, shoulder arms.*

The adjutant then goes up to the officer who is for guard, and tells him, that his guard is ready, the officer then draws his sword, and stands in front of the guard, covering the third file on the right with his sword ported. The music plays a march down the front of the guard, and back again.

As soon as the guards on the right are ready to march off, the drummer beats a signal, which is repeated by the others from right to left, and returned from left to right, on which the subaltern on the right, orders his guard to *march,* as do all the others; the bands of music of each regiment playing a slow march, when the new guard is on the line with the old one, in front of the quarter-guard tents; it is then *halted* and *dressed* by the other. The officer of the old guard orders his men to *present arms,* and the drummers beat a march, which being finished, the officer of the new guard orders his to *present arms,* the drummers likewise beating a march. The officer of the old guard recovers his sword and proceeds towards the new guard, the officer of the old guard then recovers his sword and proceeds towards the new guard, the officer of which meets him with his sword recovered; the former gives him the report in writing of the detail of the guard, names, and crimes of prisoners, and whether any thing is in charge of the guard; at the same time he drops the point of his sword, as does the other on

C receiving

receiving the report. The officers then return to the front of their guards; the old guard is ordered by its officer to *shoulder arms, order arms, ease arms*. The officer of the new guard orders his men to shoulder arms, and as soon as the corporals of both guards have taken the number requisite for relieving the sentries, the new guard receives the words of command, *order arms, ease arms*. During the relieving of the sentries the music plays. The serjeant of the new guard on receiving the report from his officer, goes through the guard tents accompanied by the serjeant of the old guard, to see the prisoners, if there are any, and what things are in the charge of the guard. On the return of the reliefs, the drummer of the old guard, on the right of the encampment, gives a signal, which is repeated by the other drummers of the old guards from right to left, and returned back. The officer of the old guard gives the following word of command. *attention, shoulder arms*, and marches them off, either by wheeling or filing, as circumstances may require, to the place of parade where he dismisses them.

The officer of the new guard, the moment the dismounting one has shouldered arms, orders his men to *shoulder arms, present arms*, and the drummer beats a march, which finished, his guard *shoulders arms*, and he *marches* it to take up the ground the other has quitted; he then *halts* and *fronts* his men, and orders them to *lodge* or pile arms.

The dismounting officer, immediately after he has dismissed his guard, presents a written report to the commanding

commanding officer of the regiment he belongs to, giving him at the fame time the parole of the former day.

The quarter-guard confifts of a fubaltern, and any number of privates, from 18 to 30—its duties are nearly fimilar to the main-guard in towns.

In garrifon, the MAIN-GUARD is either a captain's or fubaltern's guard. Both officers and men of this guard are always of the fame regiment.

The duty of this guard is to preferve the peace of the garrifon, and to receive all prifoners, whether deferters or otherwife, if there is no provoft. At the main-guard, garrifon-court-martials ufually fit.

As foon as the officer of the main-guard has mounted, he muft get a roll of the men from the ferjeant. No non-commiffioned officer or private is to quit the guard without his permiffion, and then for a limited time; to which they muft be punctual, on pain of being confined, or ftanding fentry off their turn. The roll of the guard ought to be frequently called to fee that the men are all prefent. The officer muft make the non-commiffioned officers do their duty with fpirit and regularity. As the room where the men are, is immediately under the infpection of the ferjeant, he is to be anfwerable that no noife, drinking, or gambling, be permitted there.—The officer will vifit his fentries frequently, to fee that they do their duty, and he muft know from the corporal the orders which the fentries have received.

The

The guard muſt turn out with ſhouldered arms, whenever the ſentry at the door calls, *turn out the Guard*. The officer will ſee the reaſon for it, and act accordingly. Should a general officer be approaching, he will pay him the compliment due to his rank, after which the guard will lodge their arms. If a ſentry ſhould call out the guard in a miſtake, it muſt however fall in, and be returned by the officer in a proper manner.

If a party of men in arms march paſt the guard, it will turn out; and ſhould a drum be beat, the guard is to preſent arms, and the drummer of it will beat a march. Where no drum is beat, the guard remains ſhouldered.

Whenever a crowd of people aſſemble near a guard, the men muſt be under arms, till ſuch time as the ſtreet is clear.

In caſe of fire, riots, or any diſturbance, the officer will turn out the guard, and remain at its head, till he is ordered to act by the general, commandant of the garriſon, or officer of the day.

At retreat beating, the guard muſt remain under arms, till it is finiſhed. The officer may exerciſe his guard at this time, and, if in time of war, the men muſt prime and load. The guard will turn out at reveillé beating in the morning.

The officers are not on any pretence to quit their guards, but be ready to turn out when wanted.

In wet weather bayonets ſhould not be fixed, but all the guards marched off in quick time with ſecured arm arms. In such cases no compliments pass between the guards either by drum or otherwise.

Picquet Guards

Are either a captain's or a subaltern's guard, as the nature of the service may require; they are formed exactly as the other guards, with this difference, that they do not mount till retreat beating. They are to turn out in an instant in the night, in case of alarms in camp or garrison.

The officers and men keep on their clothes and accoutrements while on duty.

Forms of sending for, and lodging the Colours.
Battalion in Line.

The commanding officer orders the grenadier drummers to beat the drummer's call, on which the two ensigns who are to carry the colours, recover their swords, face to the right, and march between the line of officers and the front rank, till they come to the head of the grenadiers, where they halt, front, and place their swords across their bodies, the points in the left hands; the drum-major with a party of drummers and fifers, will likewise face to the right, and march to the head of the grenadiers, placing themselves between the ensigns and the front rank. The captain of the grenadiers then orders his company to take *close order*, and will

either

either wheel them by fub-divifions, or march them in one. If by fub-divifions, he places himfelf on the pivot flank of the firft, the eldeft lieutenant on that of the fecond, and the other lieutenant in the fupernumerary rank of the firft; but if the company is marched in one divifion, the two lieutenants are in the fupernumerary rank: the company then *marches*, in *ordinary time*, to the quarters where the colours are lodged, when it *halts*, and *the rear ranks take open order*, the drum-major unfurls the colours and gives them out of a window to the enfigns, who on halting had fheathed their fwords. The captain of grenadiers then orders his men to *prefent arms*, the officers falute with their fwords, and the drummers beat a point of war, which finifhed he makes them *fhoulder arms*, *rear ranks take clofe order*, and *marches* them off in *ordinary time*, the drummers beating the grenadiers march. On arriving at the left flank of the regiment, the company faces to the right, the enfigns with the colours march in front of the line of officers, the grenadier officers between them and the front rank, and the grenadiers in files between the other ranks. The commanding officer of the regiment as foon as the colours arrive on the left flank, orders the battalion to *prefent arms*, the officers falute the mufic plays " God fave the King, " and the drummers beat the troop On the colours arriving in the centre of the battalion, the enfigns halt and front; and when the grenadiers have taken poft on the right, the battalion is ordered to *fhoulder arms*.

When

When the colours are to be *lodged*, on the drummer's call being beat, the enfigns, drum-major, and a party of drummers and fifers, march and take poft in front of the grenadiers. The battalion *prefent arms*, officers falute, mufic plays, and drums beat. On the captain of grenadiers marching off with the colours, the drummers beat the troop. When they arrive at the houfe or place where they are to be lodged, the drum-major receives them at a window, the grenadiers *prefent arms*, officers falute, and drummers beat a point of war. The enfigns on quitting the colours draw their fwords, and falute with the other officers. The captain will either march his company back, or difmifs them, as he may be ordered by the commanding officer.

When the colours are not to be received or lodged in form, the ferjeant major, with four ferjeants in the centre of the battalion, will take the colours cafed, from, or to the place where they are kept, in the following manner :—ferjeant-major, the two front rank ferjeants carrying the colours on their fhoulders, covered in the rear by the two other ferjeants and the drum-major, who is to receive them when they arrive at the place of their deftination. No compliment is paid by the battalion in this cafe, and they are generally fent away when the ranks are clofed.

FORM

FORM OF A REVIEW

Of a Regiment *of* British Infantry, *6co Rank and File, in* 10 *Companies, as ordered by*
HIS MAJESTY.

The march to and from the field in *column*, should be considered as one of the most material parts of exercise, and be done with attention, equality of step, just distances, and perfect order; the front of the march should be frequently increased and diminished, and the battalion at different periods formed by wheels to the flank, to shew that distances have been duly preserved.

The battalion having taken its proper ground, the following words are given:

Rear Ranks—*take open Order*.

See Plate 2d.

The colours, and officers, are 3 paces in front; captains cover the second file from the right of their companies.

Lieutenants the second from the left, and the ensigns opposite the centre of their respective companies.

The

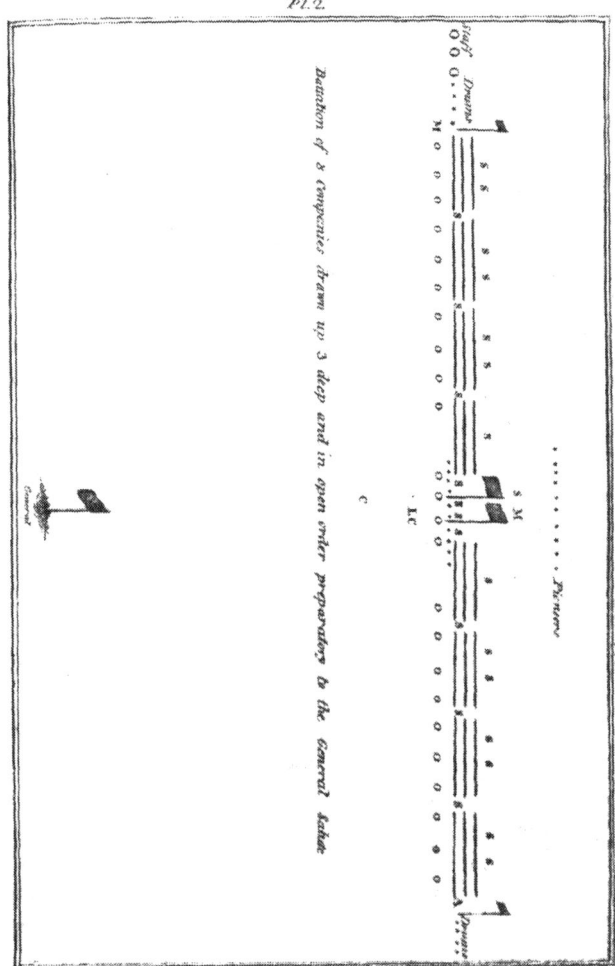

Pl. 2.

Battalion of 8 Companies drawn up 3 deep and in open order preparatory to the General Salute

The music form between the colours and the front rank.

Covering ferjeants replace their officers.

Pioneers are 6 paces behind the centre of the rear rank.

Drummers take the fame diftance behind their refpective divifions.

The major on horfe-back on the right, dreffing with the line of officers.

The adjutant mounted, is on the left, dreffing with the front rank.

The ftaff place themfelves on the right of the front rank of the grenadiers.

The lieutenant-colonel and colonel, difmounted, advance before the colours, the colonel 4 paces and the lieutenant-colonel 2 paces from them—the lieutenant-colonel in the rear of the colonel, and on his left.

The drummers, for fhow, generally are divided on the 2 flanks;—the pioneers on the right of the ftaff.

Four camp colours are to be placed fo as to form a fquare, round the angles of which the wheelings are to be made.

A fifth camp colour is to be placed 80 or 100 paces in front of the centre of the battalion, where the general is fuppofed to take his ftation; but although he may choofe to quit that pofition, ftill the colour is to be confidered as the point to which all movements and formations are relative. The colour muft be fo placed, that the right flank of the divifions, when marching

ing paſt in review, ſhall be about 4 yards diſtant from the general.

Receiving the General.

When the reviewing general is within 50 or 60 paces of the centre, he will be received with a general ſalute: the colonel, with his back to the regiment, gives the words—

Present—*Arms.*

The men preſent arms, and the officers ſalute, taking their time from the flugle man.

At the firſt motion of the *preſent*, officers recover their ſwords, at the ſecond they drop them, the muſic will play, and the drums beat.

The colours only ſalute ſuch perſons as from their rank, and by regulation, are entitled to that honour.

Shoulder—*Arms.*

The men ſhoulder, and at the firſt motion, officers recover their ſwords—at the ſecond they bring them acroſs their bodies, and remain perfectly ſteady and ſquare to the front.

While the general is going round the battalion, every perſon remains perfectly ſteady, no compliment is paid.

The muſic will play and the drums beat, they will ceaſe

ceafe as foon as the general has returned to the right flank of the battalion.

While the general is proceeding to place himfelf in the front, the colonel turns to the regiment and gives the words—

> REAR RANKS—TAKE CLOSE ORDER.
> *March.*

The colonel and lieutenant-colonel will then mount on horfeback in the rear of the centre. The colonel gives the words—

> COMPANIES, ON YOUR LEFT BACKWARDS WHEEL.
> *Quick March* *.

Pioneers and mufic are ordered to the head of the column, officers commanding companies muft be very attentive when they give the words *halt*, *drefs*, to fee that they are well obeyed.

> COLUMN—*March.*

The companies wheel fucceffively at the firft and fecond angles of the ground.

When the leading company has made the fecond wheel, it brings them on the line on which they pafs the general: each leader of a company, when it has advanced

---

* *The 1ft Regiment of Royal Edinburgh Volunteers marks time with the right, and always fteps off with the left foot. All motions on a march are performed in time; this Regiment beat with the right foot, of courfe all their motions in march are done with that only.*

advanced 6 paces from the wheeling point, changes quickly by the rear to the right flank of his company, and gives the words *eyes right*—then, REAR RANKS, *take open order*, which is done by the rear ranks marking time, one and two paces. The mufic begins to play—the officers move 3 paces in front of the company, dividing the ground equally, the captain on the right, the lieutenant on the left, and the enfign in the centre.

The captain's place is fupplied on the right flank by his covering ferjeant, who is refponfible for keeping the company at the proper wheeling diftance from the one preceding it.

The colonel is at the head of the grenadiers or leading company, with the major a little behind him on his left.

The mufic are in two ranks, 6 paces before the colonel.

The pioneers are in two ranks, 6 paces before the mufic, having a corporal at their head to lead them.

The drummers and fifers are on the left flank of their refpective companies, and the fupernumerary ferjeants 3 paces in the rear of their feveral divifions.

The lieutenant colonel is in the rear of the light company, the adjutant a little behind him on his left. The colours are 3 paces behind the 4th battalion company, covered by their ferjeants. Staff officers do not march paft.

The

The officers, when within 6 paces of the general, prepare to falute by recovering their fwords; they drop them when in a line with the general, and recover them when 10 paces from him, without in the leaft altering the rate of march, or impeding the front ranks of their companies.

The commanding officer, when he has faluted at the head of the column, places himfelf near the general, and remains there till the rear has marched paft. The drummers give a roll each, when the officers of their own companies falute.

The officers commanding companies will, each fucceffively, when he has paffed the general by 30 paces, give the words—*rear ranks, take clofe order*, and will immediately fhift to the left, the proper pivot, and each individual of the company refumes the poft which he held when the column was firft put in motion.

When the 3d wheel is completed by all the companies, and the leading company is near to where the left of the battalion ftood, the colonel gives the word—

HALT *.

The whole halt—mufic ceafes.

---

* *A change from ordinary to quick time, and from quick to ordinary, muft always be preceded by a Halt.*

Support *Arms.—Quick March.*

The whole march off in quick time.—No music †.

Marching past in Quick Time.

The column makes three several wheels, viz.—at the point where the left of the battalion first stood:— at the point where the first wheel was made, and just before making the 3d wheel, the colonel gives the word—

Carry—*Arms.*

When the 3d wheel is completed, which places the column on the line of passing the general, the music begins to play. The leading officer of each company shifts to its right by its rear, giving the word, *eyes-right,* and when he has passed the general 30 paces, he will resume his proper pivot flank, giving the word *eyes-left.*

The supernumerary officers and serjeants march in a rank, in the rear of the companies, at one pace from the rear rank, and officers swords are carried steadily against the right shoulder.

The colonel, lieutenant-colonel, major, and adjutant are in the same places as in marching past in ordinary time; as also drummers, pioneers, and music.

In marching past in quick-time, no compliment is paid by officers.

When

---

* *The use of music and drums to regulate the march is absolutely forbid, as incompatible with just movements.*

When the head of the column approaches to the left of the ground on which it originally received the general, the music will cease.

The colonel gives the words—

HALT—*March.*

The men carry their arms, and the column takes up the ordinary march, for the purpose of moving on an alignment.*

When at the point on the left of the alignment, each officer gives the words—*halt, left wheel, halt-dress* †, *march*—It is scarce necessary to observe, that these words are repeated at *every wheeling point.*

On the word *dress,* each individual will cast his eyes *to* the point to which he is ordered to dress, with the smallest turn possible of the head, but preserving the shoulders and body square to their front. The *faces* of the men, and *not* their breasts, or feet, are the line of dressing.

Each man is to be able, just, to distinguish the lower part of the face of the second man beyond him.

In dressing, the eyes of the men are *always* turned to the officer who gives the word—*dress ;* and who is posted at the point *Appui,* or *support,* by which the body halts, and who, *from* that point *Appui,* corrects his men *on* a point, at, or beyond his opposite flank, which point is called the point of FORMATION, or DRESSING.

Forming

---
* Alignment *from the French, as most of our military terms are.*
† *From the French* dresser, *to arrange.*

Forming in Line.

The column prolongs the alignment, till arrived at the point where its head or right is to be placed, viz. where it originally stood.

When the colonel sees them properly placed in the alignment, he gives the word—

Halt.

Pivots are corrected if necessary, but should be done instantly; if officers have covered correctly it will be unnecessary, and should be avoided if possible.

Left—*Wheel into Line.*

Pioneers and music go to their posts behind the centre.

Quick—*March.*

The colonel then cautions the battalion, that it will perform the manual and platoon exercise, he immediately goes to the rear, and the major advances to the front of the battalion, and gives the words of command.

Rear Ranks, take open Order.

March.

Order—*Arms.*

Unfix—*Bayonets.*

Shoulder

SHOULDER—*Arms.*

OFFICERS—*Take post in the Rear.*

Officers recover their swords and face to the right.

March.

Officers, colours, &c. march through the several intervals occupied by the serjeants, 3 paces beyond the rear rank.

Front.

The officers front, and bring their swords to the port.

The commanding officer, lieutenant-colonel, adjutant, pioneers, music, supernumerary serjeants, drummers, and fifers, are at their posts in the rear, as when the battalion is formed at close order, where they remain perfectly steady.

The major proceeds with the manual as *directed* by regulation, observing that the front rank only comes down to the *last* position of the charge bayonets, the others remain ported. The serjeants who preserve in the front rank the places of the platoon officers remain there steady during the whole of the manual, except that they charge their pikes at the same time as the bayonets.

MANUAL

*MANUAL EXERCISE.

I. Order—*Arms*—3 *motions*.

Bring the firelock to the trail in two motions as usual, seizing it at the first at the lower loop, just above the swell; at the second, bring it down to the right side, the butt within two inches of the ground: at the third, drop the butt on the ground, placing the muzzle against the hollow of the right shoulder, and the hand flat upon the sling.

II. Fix, &c.—1 *motion*.

At the word *fix*, place the thumb of the right hand, as quick as possible, behind the barrel, taking a gripe of the firelock; as soon as the word of command is fully out, push the firelock a little forward, at the same time drawing out the bayonet with the left hand, and fixing it with the utmost celerity:—The instant this is done, return, as quick as possible, to the *order*, as above described, and stand perfectly steady.

III.

---

* *Although the Manual and Platoon Exercises form no part of a Review, as they are sometimes ordered, we shall here insert the words of command, and directions how to perform the several motions. The Flugle man gives the Time with his back to the Battalion.*

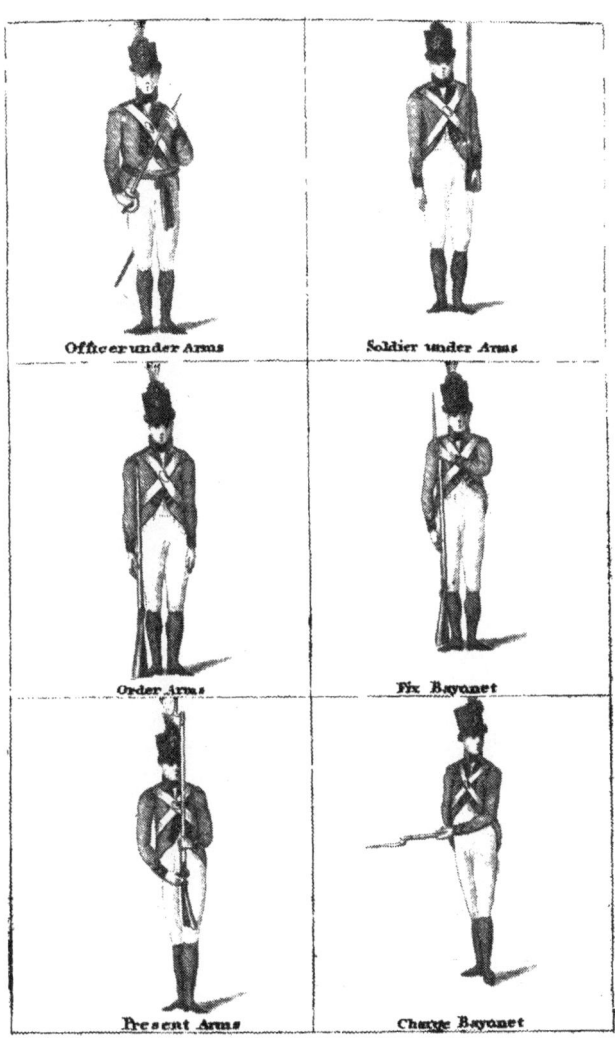

MANUAL EXER

III. SHOULDER—*Arms*—1 *motion.*

As soon as the word *shoulder* is given, take a gripe of the firelock with the right hand, as in fixing bayonets, and at the laft word, *arms*, the firelock muft be thrown with the right hand, in one motion, and with as little appearance of effort as poffible, into its proper pofition on the left fhoulder;—the hand croffes the body in fo doing, but muft inftantly be withdrawn.

IV. PRESENT—*Arms*—3 *motions.*

1ft. Seize the firelock with the right hand, under the guard, turning the lock to the front, but without moving it from the fhoulder.

2d. Bring it to the *poize*, feizing it with the left hand, the fingers extended along the fling, the wrift upon the guard, and the point of the left thumb of equal height with the eyes.

3d. Bring down the firelock with a quick motion, as low as the right hand will admit without reftraint, drawing back the right foot at the fame inftant, fo that the hollow of it may touch the left heel.—The firelock in this pofition is to be totally fupported in the left hand;—the body to reft entirely on the left foot— both knees to be ftraight.

V. SHOULDER—*Arms*—2 *motions.*

1ft. By a turn of the right wrift, bring the firelock to its proper pofition on the fhoulder, as defcribed above,

above, the left hand grafping the butt:—2d. Quit the right hand, bring it brifkly down to its place by the fide.

VI. Charge—*Bayonets*—2 *motions.*

1ft. At one motion throw the firelock from the fhoulder, acrofs the body, to a low diagonal recover, a pofition known in many regiments by the name of *porting arms,* or, *preparing for the charge,* in which the lock is to be turned to the front, and at the height of the breaft; the muzzle flanting upwards, fo that the barrel may crofs oppofite the point of the left fhoulder, with the butt proportionally depreffed; the right hand grafps the fmall of the butt, and the left holds the piece at the fwell, clofe to the lower pipe, the thumbs of both hands pointing towards the muzzle.

2d. Make a half face to the right, and bring down the firelock to nearly a horizontal pofition, with the muzzle inclining a little upwards, and the right wrift refting againft the hollow of the thigh, juft below the hip.

The firft motion of the *charge* is the pofition which the foldier will, either from the fhoulder, or after firing, take, in order to advance on an enemy, whom it is intended to attack with fixed bayonets; and the word of command for that purpofe is " *prepare to charge.*" The fecond pofition of the charge is that which the front rank takes when arrived at a few yards diftance from the body to be attacked. The firft first motion of the *charge* is also that which sentries are to take when challenging any persons who approach their posts *.

VII. Shoulder—*Arms*—2 *motions*.

1st. Face to the front, and throw up the piece into its position on the shoulder, by a turn of the right wrist, instantly grasping the butt, as above described, with the left hand.

2d. Quit the firelock briskly with the right hand, bringing it to its proper place by the side.

Here ends the manual; but the men ought to have learned likewise *to support arms* at *three* motions, throwing the first and second nearly into one: at the first motion they seize the small of the butt under the lock with the right hand, bringing the butt in the front of the groin, and keeping the lock somewhat turned out: at the second they bring the left arm under the cock: at the third they quit the right hand. In *carrying arms* from the *support*, the motions are exactly reversed.

In marching any distance, or in standing at ease, when *supported*, the men are allowed to bring their right hand across the body, to the small of the butt, which latter must, in that case, be thrown still more forward; the fingers of the left hand being uppermost, must be placed between the body and the right elbow:

* *See the Frontispiece.*

elbow: the right hands are to be instantly removed, when the division *halts*, or is ordered to *dress by the right*.

Time.

Three seconds between each motion, except that of *fixed bayonets*, in which a longer time must be given.

In regard to the motions of *securing, grounding*, and *trailing*, as well as those of *piling*, &c. it will be sufficient for the soldiers to be taught to perform them in the most convenient and quickest method. *Returning bayonets* is to be done from the *order*, in the same manner as *fixing* them.

Sentries.

Sentries posted with shouldered arms, are permitted afterwards to *support*, but not to slope them.—On the approach of an officer, they immediately *carry* their arms and put themselves into their proper position; which is not to be done at the instant he passes, but by the time he is within twenty yards of their post, so that they may be perfectly steady before he comes up.

Corporals.

Corporals marching with reliefs, or commanding detachments, or divisions, will carry their arms *advanced*, as at present; for which purpose a soldier, when promoted to that rank, must be taught the position of *advanced arms*.

ADVANCE

Advance—*Arms*—3 *Motions.*

1ft. Spring the firelock to the poife.

2d. Bring it fmartly clofe to the front of the right fhoulder, finking it at the fame time as low as the right hand will admit, which holds the piece firm under the guard.

3d. The left hand which had been thrown acrofs the body, and as high as the right fhoulder, to fteady and fix the firelock in a perpendicular pofition, is then withdrawn quickly to the left thigh;—in this pofition the firelock is fupported entirely by the right hand, with the fling to the front.

Secure—*Arms*—3 *Motions.*
From the Shoulder.

1ft. Seize the firelock with the right hand under the guard, as in the firft motion of fupporting arms.

2d. Throw up the left hand, and gripe the piece under the fwell.

3d. Quit the right hand and bring the firelock with the left under your left arm, the barrel downwards, and the muzzle within a foot of the ground, taking care to fecure the lock from the wet.

Ground—*Arms.*
From the order—4 *Motions.*

1ft. Seize the top of the firelock brifkly with the right hand—

2. Turn

2. Turn it till the lock is brought to the rear, at the same time making a half face to the right, turn the right foot and place it against the flat side of the butt, the toe pointing directly to the right.

3d. Step directly forward a moderate pace with the left foot, slipping down the right hand at the same time to the middle of the barrel; lay the firelock on the ground in a straight line to the front, the lock upwards.

4th. Rise briskly up again, bringing back the left foot to its former place, turn the right foot on the heel over the but end, bringing the body at the same time to its proper front, the hands down by each side.

In taking up the firelock the above motions are reversed.

In laying down and taking up the firelocks, the soldiers are to keep their heads well up, and not step too far with their left feet, that they may with the more ease recover themselves.

Piling Arms.

Three firelocks are placed with their butts wide asunder, and forming a triangle; the tops are inclined inwards and locked together either by the ramrods or the bayonets; the piles must stand firm on the ground, the locks all turned outwards.

Sloping Arms.

The firelock rests on the left shoulder, the muzzle raised—this is permitted on a long march.

PLA

PLATOON EXERCISE.*

(See the Plates.)

Words of Command.

I. MAKE—*Ready*—1 *Motion.*

SPRING the firelock to the *recover*, and instantly cocking,

II. PRESENT—1 *Motion.*

Slip the left hand along the sling as far as the swell of the firelock, and bring the piece down to the *present*, stepping back about six inches to the rear with the right foot.

III. FIRE—1 *Motion.*

After firing drop the firelock briskly to the *priming* position and half cock.

IV. HANDLE—*Cartridge*—2 *Motions.*

1st. Draw the cartridge from the pouch.
2d. Bring it to the mouth, holding it between the fore-finger and thumb, and bite off the top of it.

The platoon exercise is always done at close order, except at drill

V. PRIME—3 *Motions.*

1ſt. Shake ſome powder into the pan.

2d. Shut the pan with the three laſt fingers.

3d. Seize the ſmall of the butt with the above three fingers.

VI. LOAD—3 *Motions.*

1ſt. Face to the left on both heels, ſo that the right toe may point directly to the front, and the body be a very little faced to the left, bringing at the ſame time the firelock round to the left ſide without ſinking it. It ſhould, in this momentary poſition, be almoſt perpendicular, having the muzzle only a ſmall degree brought forward, and as ſoon as it is ſteady there, it muſt inſtantly be forced down within two inches of the ground, the butt nearly oppoſite the left heel, and the firelock itſelf ſomewhat ſlopped, and directly to the front; the right hand at the ſame inſtant catches the muzzle, in order to ſteady it.

2d. Shake the powder into the barrel, putting in after it the paper and ball.

3d. Seize the top of the ramrod, with the forefinger and thumb.

VII. DRAW—*Ramrods*—2 *Motions.*

1ſt Force the ramrod half out, and ſeize it backhanded exactly in the middle.

2d. Draw it entirely out, and turning it with the

whole

whole hand and arm extended from you, put it one inch into the barrel.

VIII. RAM-DOWN—*Cartridge*—4 *Motions.*

1st. Push the ramrod down, holding it as before, exactly in the middle, till the hand touches the muzzle.

2d. Slip the fore-finger and thumb to the upper end, without letting the ramrod fall farther into the barrel.

3d. Push the cartridge well down to the bottom.

4th. Strike it two very quick strokes with the ramrod.

IX. RETURN—*Ramrods*—2 *Motions.*

1st. Draw the ramrod half out, catching it back-handed.

2d. Draw it entirely out, turning it very briskly from you, with the arm extended, and put into the loops, forcing it as quick as possible to the bottom; then face to the proper front, the finger and thumb of the right hand holding the ramrod, as in the position immediately previous to drawing it, and the butt raised two inches from the ground.

X. SHOULDER—*Arms*—1 *Motion.*

Strike top of the muzzle smartly with the right hand, in order to fix the bayonet, and ramrod, more firmly, and at the same time throw it nimbly up, at one motion to the shoulder.

N. B.

---

* *The 1st Regiment R. E. V. on parade shoulder the old way, by three motions.*

N. B. Though the butts are not to come to the ground in casting about, as accidents may happen from it, yet they are permitted, while loading, to be so rested; but it must be done without noise, and in a manner imperceptible in the front.

Explanation of Priming and Loading quick.

Words of Command—*Prime and Load.*

1st. Bring the firelock down in one brisk motion to the priming position, the thumb of the right hand placed against the pan-cover, or steel; the fingers clenched; and the elbow a little turned out, so that the wrist may be clear of the cock.

2d. Open the pan, by throwing up the steel, with a strong motion of the right arm, turning the elbow in, and keeping the firelock steady in the left hand.

3d. Bring your hand round to the pouch, and draw out the cartridge.

The rest as above described, excepting that, in the quick loading, all the motions are to be done with as much dispatch as possible; the soldiers taking their time from the flugle man in front, for *casting over and shouldering only.*

In firing three deep, the priming position for the front rank is the height of the waistband of the breeches: for the centre rank, about the middle of the stomach: and for the rear rank, close to the breast:

the

he firelock, in all these positions, is to be kept perfect-horizontal.

Explanation of the Position of each Rank in the Firings.

As Front Rank kneeling.

Make Ready.

BRING the firelock briskly up to the *recover*, catching it in the left hand; and without stopping, sink down with a quick motion upon the right knee, keeping the left foot fast, the butt end of the firelock, at the same moment, falling upon the ground; then cock, and instantly seize the cock and steel together in the right hand, holding the piece firm in the left, about the middle of that part, which is between the lock and the swell of the stock: the point of the left thumb to be close to the swell, and pointing upwards.

As the body is sinking, the right knee is to be thrown so far back that the left leg may be right up and down, the right foot a little turned out, the body straight, and the head as much up as if shouldered; the firelock must be upright, and the butt about four inches to the right of the inside of the left foot.

Present.

Bring the firelock down firmly to the *present*, by sliding the left hand to the full extent of the arm, along the sling, without letting the motion tell;—the right

right hand at the fame time fpringing up the butt by the cock fo high againſt the right ſhoulder, that the head may not be too much lowered in taking aim; the right cheek to be clofe to the butt; the left eye ſhut, and the middle finger of the right hand on the trigger, look along the barrel with the right eye from the breech pin to the muzzle, and remain ſteady.

Fire.

Pull the trigger ſtrong with the middle finger, and, as foon as fired, ſpring up nimbly upon the left leg, keeping the body erect and the left foot faſt, and bringing the right heel to the hollow of the left; at the fame inſtant drop the firelock to the priming pofition, the height of the waiſtband of the breeches; *half cock, handle caatridge*, and go on with the loading motions as before defcribed.

AS CENTRE RANK.

Make ready.

SPRING the firelock briſkly to the *recover*; as foon as the left hand feizes the firelock above the lock, raife the right elbow a little, placing the thumb of that hand upon the cock, with the fingers open on the plate of the lock, and then, as quick as poffible, cock the piece, by dropping the elbow, and forcing down the cock with the thumb, ſtep at the fame time with the right foot a moderate pace to the right, and keeping

ing the left faſt, ſeize the ſmall of the butt with the right hand: the piece muſt be held in this poſition perpendicular, and oppoſite the left ſide of the face, the butt cloſe to the breaſt, but not preſſed, the body ſtraight, and full to the front, and the head erect.

Preſent.

As in the foregoing explanation for the front rank.

Fire.

Pull the trigger ſtrong with the middle finger, and, as ſoon as fired, bring the firelock to the priming poſition, about the height of the ſtomach; the reſt, as in explanation of *priming* and *loading*—with this difference only, that the left foot is to be drawn up to the right, at the ſame time that the firelock is brought down to the priming poſition; and that, immediately after the firelock is thrown up to the ſhoulder, the men ſpring to the left again, and cover their file leaders.

AS REAR RANK.

Make ready.

RECOVER and cock, as before directed from the centre rank, and, as the firelock is brought to the recover, ſtep briſkly to the right a full pace, at the ſame time placing the left heel about ſix inches before the point of the right foot.—The body to be kept ſtraight, and as ſquare to the front as poſſible.

Preſent

Present.

As in explanation for the centre rank.

Fire.

As in explanation for the centre rank, remembering only, the difference of the priming position for this rank, as before described; after firing and shouldering, the men step as the centre rank does.

In firing with the front rank *standing*, that rank makes ready, &c. as specified in the article relative to the *platoon exercise*.

OFFICERS,

FIRING BY PLATOONS,

INSTEAD of giving the words, *platoon, make ready, present*, are to pronounce the words short, as for instance, *toon, ready, pfent.*

In firing by platoons, or divisions, the officers commanding them are to step out one pace, on the close of the *preparative*, and face to the left towards their men: they there stand perfectly steady till the last part of the *general*, when they step back again into their proper intervals, all at the same time.—After a division has fired, the right-hand man of it steps out one pace, in front of the officer, but still keeping his own proper front, and gives the time for *casting about* and *shouldering,*

Table

Showing at one View the Firings of 8 Companies by Grand Divisions Companies & Sub-divisions

Pl.3.

Fire twice by Grand Divisions from Right to Left														
1				2				3				4			
5				6				7				8			

Fire twice by Grand Divisions from Left to Right														
4				3				2				1			
8				7				6				5			

Fire twice by Compy from Right to Left															
1		2		3		4		5		6		7		8	
9		10		11		12		13		14		15		16	

Fire twice by Compy from Left to Right															
8		7		6		5		4		3		2		1	
16		15		14		13		12		11		10		9	

Fire twice by Compy from Center to Flanks															
7		5		3		1		2		4		6		8	
15		13		11		9		10		12		14		16	

Fire twice by Compy from Flanks to Center															
1		3		5		7		8		6		4		2	
9		11		13		15		16		14		12		10	

Fire twice by Sub-divisions from Flanks to Center															
1	3	5	7	9	11	13	15	16	14	12	10	8	6	4	2
17	19	21	23	25	27	29	31	32	30	28	26	24	22	20	18

Fire twice by Sub-divisions from Center to Flanks															
15	13	11	9	7	5	3	1	2	4	6	8	10	12	14	16
31	29	27	25	23	21	19	17	18	20	22	24	26	28	30	32

The Numbers next to this Line represent the evolution Compy and those next the double Line the Right Center Compy's Odd divisions

The Numbers next to this Line represent the Light Infantry Compy and those next the double Line the Left Center Compy's Sub-divisions

The Double middle Line marks the Center of the Battalion

shouldering, after which, he falls back again into his place in the front rank.

In firing by grand divisions, the centre officer falls back, on the *preparative*, into the fourth rank, and is replaced by the covering serjeant.

The annexed table will shew distinctly the firings of ight companies.

(See Plate 3d.)

For more particulars of this important part of the soldier's duty, see page 13. &c.

Method of Performing the Eighteen Manoeuvres ordred for a Review.

First Manoeuvre.

Close Column on a Rear Division.

(Plates 4, 5, 6, & 7.)

Form close column of companies in rear of the grenadiers *.

Form close column of two companies, *i. e.* in grand-divisions.

Face and march to the right.

Deploy

Right Grenadiers First Regiment of Royal Edinburgh Volunteers.

Deploy on the rear division.

The column marches quick 20 or 30 paces to the right, and without halting, begins to deploy into line on the rear division. The commander of the battalion gives the word for each grand-division to *halt, front.*

The whole is performed in the following manner:
The commanding officer gives the

CAUTION.

1st. The battalion will form a close column of companies in rear of the grenadiers.

REMAINING COMPANIES,
RIGHT—*Face.*

All the companies, except the grenadiers, face to the right. The officers commanding companies, and their covering serjeants, post themselves at the head of their files ready to lead, two or three leading files of each company disengage a little to the right.

The officer commanding the grenadier company, with his covering serjeant, shifts to the left of his company, the pivot flank. The commanding officer then gives the word—

QUICK—*March.*

All the companies, except the grenadiers, step off at once, and move on in file*, till they come near

the

* *After* facing, *and at the word* march, *the whole division steps off at the same instant,* 30 *inches, each man replacing, or rather over-stepping the foot*

the company to be formed on, when the ſerjeants who were leading the files ſtep briſkly forward to mark the ſituation of their companies in the perpendicular of the front of the column, the covering ſerjeant of the firſt company, halts one pace in the rear of the covering ſerjeant of the grenadier company, carefully covering him, and ſtanding perfectly ſquare in his own perſon, his own officer alſo halts cloſe to him, and allows his company to move on in the rear of the ſerjeant, taking care that the right-hand or leading file of the company, does not paſs beyond, but mark time when he comes up to the right-hand file of the grenadiers; as ſoon therefore as the officer ſees that the left-hand file of his company is in with his covering ſerjeant, he inſtantly gives the word, *half front, eyes-left*; and having dreſſed his company correctly, on his covering-ſerjeant, he gives the word—*eyes front*, takes his proper poſt which his ſerjeant had kept for him, who immediately covers him, while the officer himſelf correctly covers

---

foot of the man before him; that is, the right foot of the ſecond man comes within the left foot of the firſt, and thus of every one, more or leſs, overlapping, according to the cloſeneſs or openneſs of the files, and the length of ſtep.—This is called locking up—each ſoldier muſt look along the necks of thoſe before him, and never to right or left; *otherwiſe a waving of the march will take place, and of courſe, the loſs and extenſion of the line, and diſtance, whenever the body returns to its proper front. The ſame poſition of feet as above, takes place alſo in all marching in front, where the ranks are cloſe and locked up.*

The ſtricteſt obſervance of all the rules for marching is particularly neceſſary in marching by files, the Lock *or* Deploy *ſtep.*

vers the officer and covering serjeant of the grenadier company.

In this manner each succeeding company proceeds till the column is completely formed.

The colours precede the 5th company, and remain on its reverse flank, covered by their serjeants.

The close column is now formed, with the right in front.

(Plate 4.)

The commanding officer gives the

CAUTION,

FORM COLUMN OF GRAND DIVISIONS.

At this caution, all supernumeraries, *but not the colours*, go to the rear of the column, if not there already.

LEFT COMPANIES.

LEFT—*Face*.

The left companies immediately face, always to the pivot flank, and their officers take one side step to the right, so as to be clear of their rank.

March.

(Plate 5)

The officers stand fast, the serjeant conducts the divisions, and the officer of each, when it has cleared the

1st Manœuvre. *Pl. 4.*

The Battalion forming close column of companies behind the Grenadiers the right in front.

1.ᵗ Manœuvre.   Pl. 5.

The left or alternate Comp.ˢ wheeling out in file to form column of Grand divisions

The General

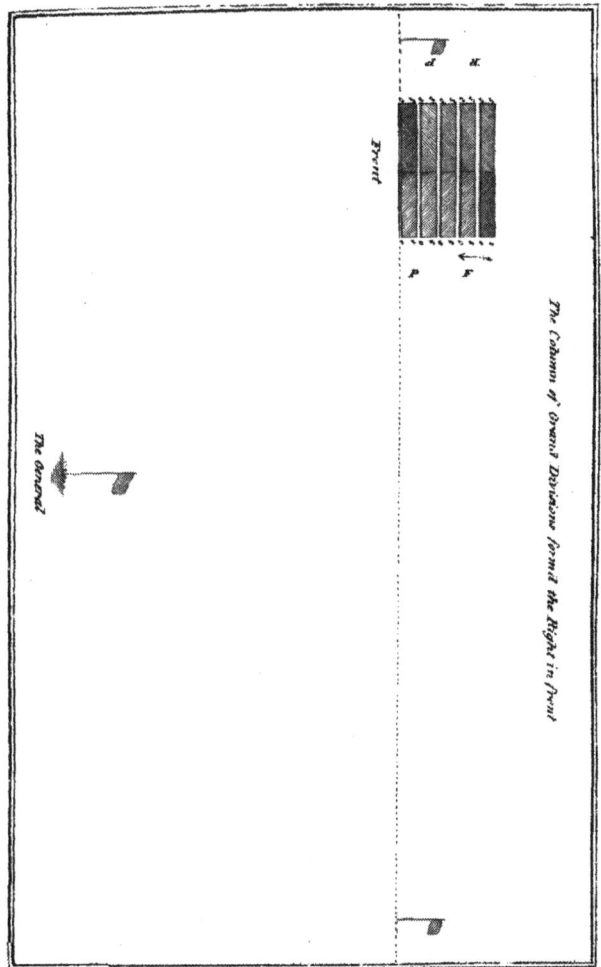

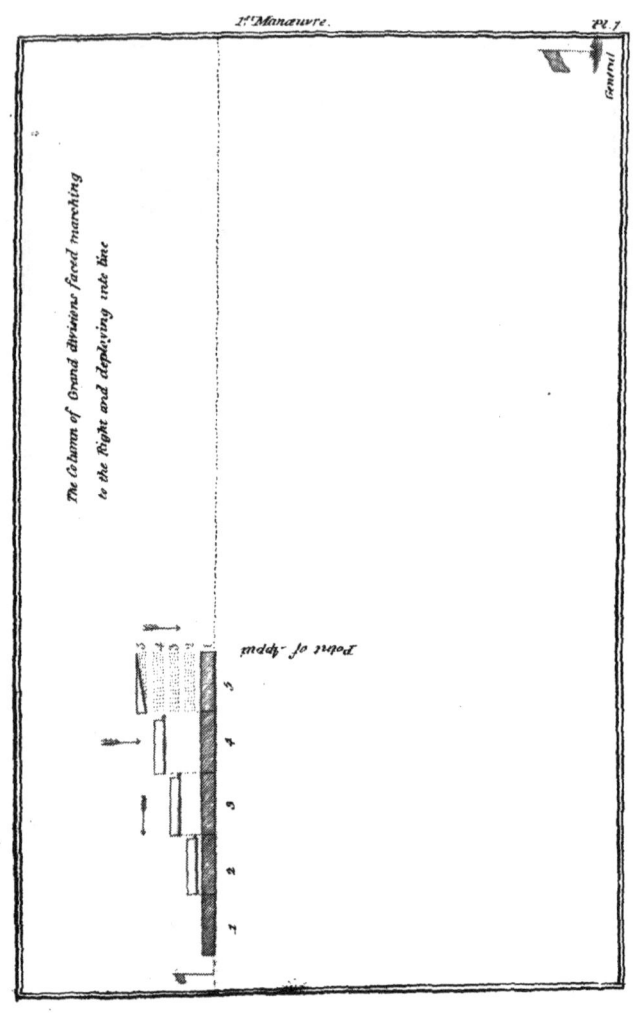

1st Manœuvre.

The Column of Grand divisions faced marching to the Right and deploying into line

(61)

the standing division, gives the word, *halt-front dress*— he then steps nimbly to the 3d file of the standing company, and *from* that gives the word, *march-halt-dress*.

(Plate 6.)

The officers commanding the *right* companies are now on the *right* of each grand-division, the officers commanding the left companies are on the *left* of each grand division, their intervals being kept by their serjeants.

CAUTION.

COLUMN WILL CLOSE TO THE FRONT.

March.

All the divisions step off, except the front one, and each division, when within one pace of the division in its front, gets the word, *halt-dress*, from the pivot officer of each division. The close column of grand-divisions is now formed, and ready to march or deploy.

(Plate 7.)

The colours are with their proper division in the column, and that division must of course out-flank on the hand, not the pivot [*].

F   The

---

[*] *Some regiments leave a space between the 3d and 4th grand divisions for the colours to prevent the out-flanking.*

The commanding officer then gives the

CAUTION.

THE COLUMN WILL TAKE GROUND TO THE RIGHT, AND ON THE MARCH DEPLOY ON THE REAR GRAND-DIVISION.

At this caution, a serjeant immediately steps out from the rear division, and places himself on the pivot flank of the front grand-division, when the rear grand-division is halted, this serjeant halts also, and instantly fronts, remaining perfectly steady to mark the ground for the rear grand-division to march up to.

The commanding officer then gives the

CAUTION,

RIGHT—*Face*.

The column faces to the right.

QUICK—*March*.

When the column has marched as far as the commanding officer sees necessary, generally 20 or 30 paces, he gives the

CAUTION,

REAR GRAND-DIVISIONS,

HALT—*Front*.

When

When he sees that the division immediately before the rear one has cleared its front, he gives the

CAUTION,

FOURTH GRAND-DIVISION,

HALT—*Front*.

And so of all the rest.

As soon as the rear grand-division, after it has received the word *halt-front*, finds its flank free by the *halt-front* of the division that was immediately before it, at that instant the officer *on the left*, gives it the word *march*.

The grand division marches steadily till it places its pivot flank, the left, close to the serjeant who had stept out to mark the ground for it; it then receives the word, *halt-dress*, from the officer on the *left*, he dresses the grand-division, *from* the standing serjeant, *the point of Appui* *, to the camp colour, the point of *formation*, on the right; as soon as the dressing is finished, he shifts to the right of his company.

The rear grand division being dressed, the grand-division next to it is marched up and dressed on it, exactly as the rear one had dressed on the standing serjeant, and so division after division, till all are in line. If the deployment be correctly made, the 1st

grand-

* Appui, or support, *means that point where the leading flank of the body is to rest.*

grand divifion has only to *Halt-Front*, as it is already in the true line.

Much of the exactnefs of this, and every deployment of the fame kind, muft depend on the accuracy of the mounted officer, who halts and fronts each grand-divifion; for this purpofe he muft be in the rear of the column. If he is confufed, all will be deranged.

Supernumerary officers and ferjeants, drums, mufic and pioneers, halt with their refpective grand divifions, and as they are *Halted* and *Dreffed* take their proper ftations in the rear

The line is now formed to the general's left.

Obferve—When the column deploys on the rear-divifion it faces from the pivot flank, which then becomes the following one.

Second Manoeuvre.

(See Plates 8, 9, & 10.)

Close Column on a Front Division.

FORM clofe column of companies in front of the left.

Form clofe column of two companies.

Face and march to the left.

Deploy on the front divifion.

The

2nd Manœuvre.

Battalion forming close column of Companies in the front of the Light Infantry, the Right in front

The column marches quick 30 or 40 paces to the left, and without halting begins to deploy on the front division.

The commanding officer of the battalion gives the word for each division to *Halt, Front.*

The whole is performed in the following manner:

The commanding officer gives the

CAUTION.

THE BATTALION WILL FORM CLOSE COLUMN OF COMPANIES IN FRONT OF THE LIGHT INFANTRY.*

(See plate 8.)

REMAINING COMPANIES,

LEFT—*Face.*

The officers commanding companies and their covering serjeants, post themselves at the head of their leading files, heads of files disengage.

QUICK—*March.*

The covering serjeant of the 8th company steps briskly forward till he comes in *front* of the light infantry officer, and three paces from him, he faces him,

---

* *In the 1st Regiment of R. E. V. left grenadiers, that regiment having no light infantry.*

him, then being certain that he is in a true line with him.--he immediately goes to the right about, and stands perfectly steady and square to his front. The officer leads on the company till he places his pivot-man close to the serjeant; he then gives the word, *Halt, Front-Dress*, replaces his serjeant, who immediately covers him, and then the officer gives the word, *Eyes Front*.

In this manner each succeeding company proceeds till the column is completely formed.

The colours move in rear of the 5th company.

The column of grand-divisions is formed and closed up, exactly as directed in the first manœuvre.

The commanding officer then gives the

CAUTION.

THE COLUMN WILL TAKE GROUND TO THE LEFT AND ON THE MARCH DEPLOY ON THE FRONT GRAND-DIVISION.

(See Plates 9 & 10.)

LEFT—*Face*.

The column faces to the left.

QUICK—*March*.

When the column has marched 30 or 40 paces, then the commanding officer gives successively, and in due time, to each grand-division, the word *Halt-Front*.

2nd Manœuvre   Pl. 9

Point of Appui

The Column of Grand Divisions deploying to the left to form the line.

Original Line

The General

Point of Formation

2nd Manœuvre.   Pl. 10.

The Column of Grand Division deployed to left into line

The General

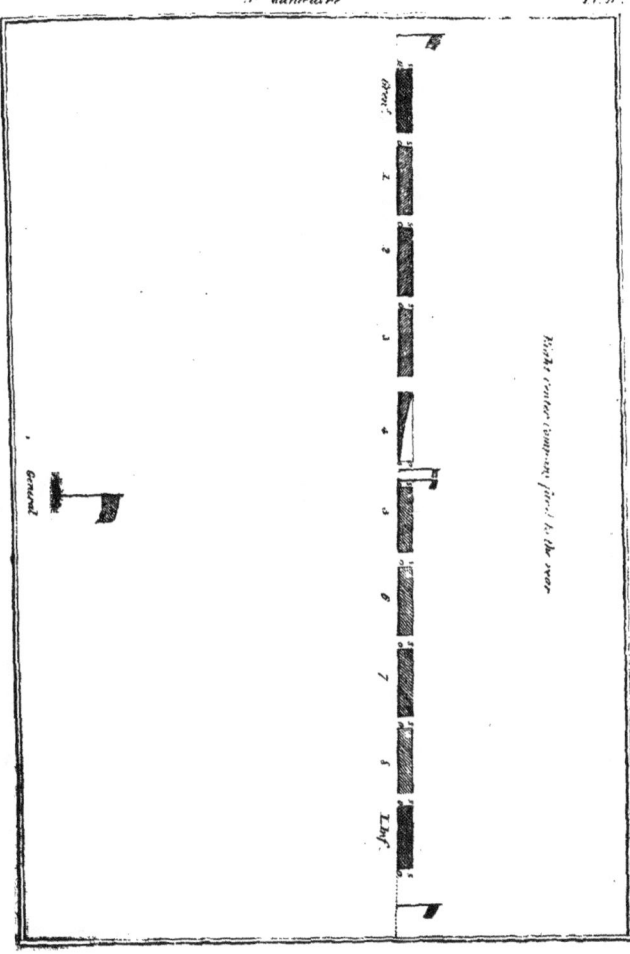

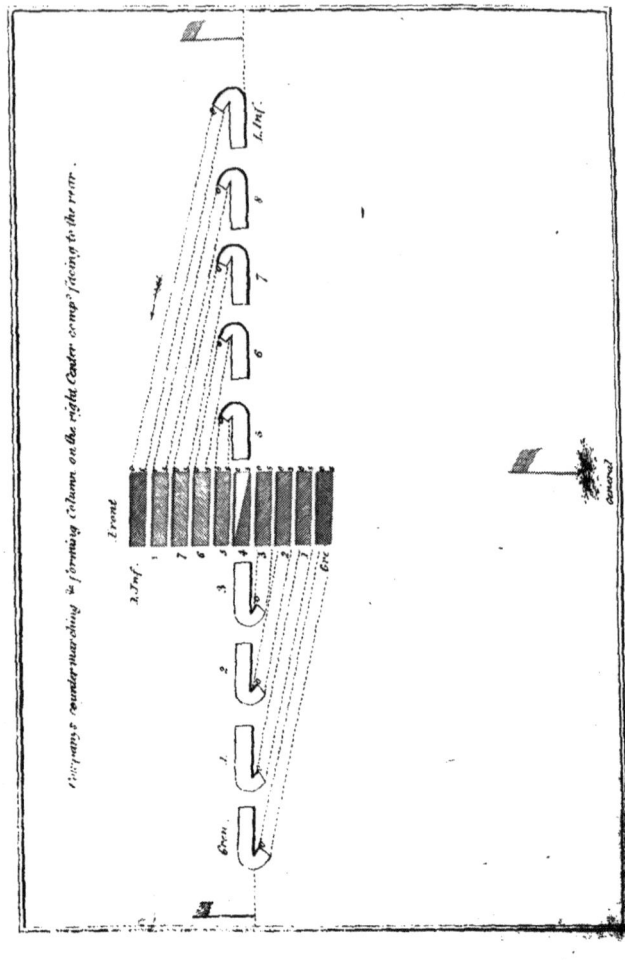

3rd Manœuvre. Pl. 13.

Point of Formation

L.Inf.

Grend.

Columns faced to the left & Counter Marching on its own Ground to bring its right in front

The General

Point of Formation

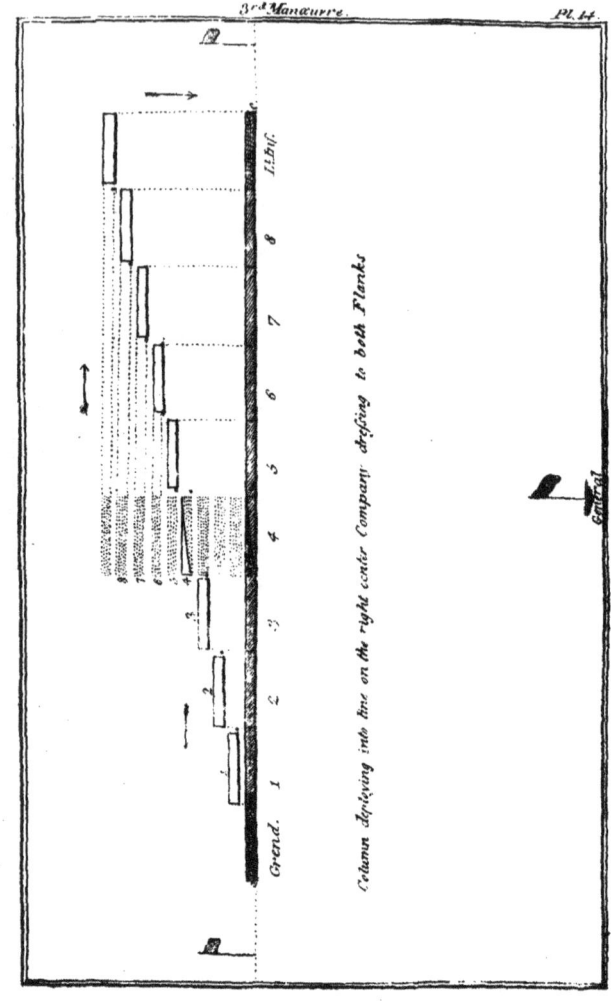

Front. The inward officer of each grand-division, that is the officer on the right, when it has halted and fronted, gives his words, *Dress, March, Halt-Dress*, and the outward officer, that is the officer on the left, remains on the flank of the division in the line, till the succeeding officer, having so dressed his grand division, comes to replace him; he, (the officer on the left) then replaces his covering serjeant on the right of his proper company.

In this manner, division after division comes up into line, and the supernumeraries, &c. also gradually take their place in the rear.

Observe—When the column deploys on a front division, it faces *to* the pivot flank, which then becomes the leading one.

Third Manoeuvre.

Close Column on a central Division facing to the Rear.

(See Plates 11, 12, 13 & 14.

FORM close column of companies on a central company, either flank in front, and facing to the rear.

Countermarch of each division in close column.

Deploy on any central named company.

The close column is formed facing to the rear, it then countermarches each division, so as to return to

the

the proper front. In the central deployment by companies, the company officers give the words to *Halt-Front*.

The whole is performed in the following manner:

The commanding officer gives the

CAUTION.

THE BATTALION WILL FORM A CLOSE COLUMN ON THE RIGHT CENTRE COMPANY, FACING TO THE REAR.

(See Plate 11.)

RIGHT CENTRE COMPANY,

RIGHT—*Face*.

The company immediately faces to the right.

RIGHT—COUNTERMARCH.

QUICK—*March*.

As soon as it has countermarched, its own officer gives it the words, *Halt-Front, Dress* by the rear rank of the 5th company; he is then on his pivot flank, the right of the company. The colours and centre serjeants countermarch with this company.

Remaining Companies.

Outwards—*Face.*

The companies on the right of the right centre company, face to the right, those on the left of it face to the left, officers and covering serjeants move to the head of the files.

To the left—Countermarch.

(Plate 12.)

Quick—*March.*

The officers lead the files, the whole step off at once; the companies of the left-wing, No. 5, 6, 7, 8, and light infantry, file one after another in the front of the right centre company. The right wing, No. 1, 2, 3, and grenadiers, file one after another into the rear of the right centre company, the serjeants must be very careful to follow the instructions as in the 1st. and 2d. manœuvre.

Each company as it completes its countermarch, receives the words, *Halt-Front, Dress,* from its own officer, who is now on the pivot-flank, the right.

The column now stands facing to the rear, with its left in front.

Column.

Left—*Face.*

The column immediately faces to the left, officers, &c. move to the heads of files to lead them. *All the covering serjeants stand fast,*

The left companies will lead out.

Quick—*March.*

The left or alternate companies, that is, No. 1, 3, 5, 7, light infantry, march out in quick time; when they have cleared the standing companies about 4 or five paces, the colonel gives the word—

Halt.

Caution.

The whole will countermarch to the left.

To the left—Countermarch.

(See Plate 13.)

Quick—*March.*

The whole, except the covering serjeants, who face to the right about, instantly countermarch, the *right* companies, *i. e.* grenadiers, 2d, 4th, 6th, 8th, countermarch on their own ground exactly. The left companies

companies, 1st, 3d, 5th, 7th, light-infantry, continue their march until they fill the intervals they had quitted. The officers of each company give the words, *Halt-Front, Dress,* as their companies finish the countermarch, which is compleated when the leading man of each front rank arrives at his respective serjeant.

When the countermarch is finished, the column stands with its right in front, as in the 1st manœuvre, and its centre opposite the general.

Caution.

The Column will deploy on the right centre Company.

(See Plate 14.)

The right centre company stands fast.

Remaining Companies,

Outwards—*Face.*

The companies on the right of the right centre, face to the right, those on the left of it, face to the left.

Quick—*March.*

The covering serjeant of the right centre company steps up to the left flank of the grenadiers, and remains there: as soon as the flanks of the right-centre company are clear, the officer commanding it gives

the

the word *March*, and when he arrives close to his covering serjeant, who occupies the exact ground quitted by the grenadier officer, he then with great correctness *Halts* and *Dresses* his company on the serjeant, to the point of formation on the right, and then giving the words, *Eyes Front*, shifts to the right of his company.

When the remaining companies are clear of each other's flanks, they get the words, *Halt-Front, March*, from their own officers. The 3d company dresses from the *right* of the right centre company, its point of *Appui*, to the distant point of formation on the right, the other companies of the right-wing dress in the same manner on the standing companies as they severally come up into line.

When the 5th, or left centre company, has marched up to its point of *Appui*, the left flank of the right centre company, its officer *from* that point dresses his company *to* the point of formation on the *left*.

In this manner each company proceeds till all are in line on their original ground, the centre opposite the general.

Some Necessary Observations relative to the Column.

When the divisions that compose a battalion, stand the one directly behind the other, that corps is then
in

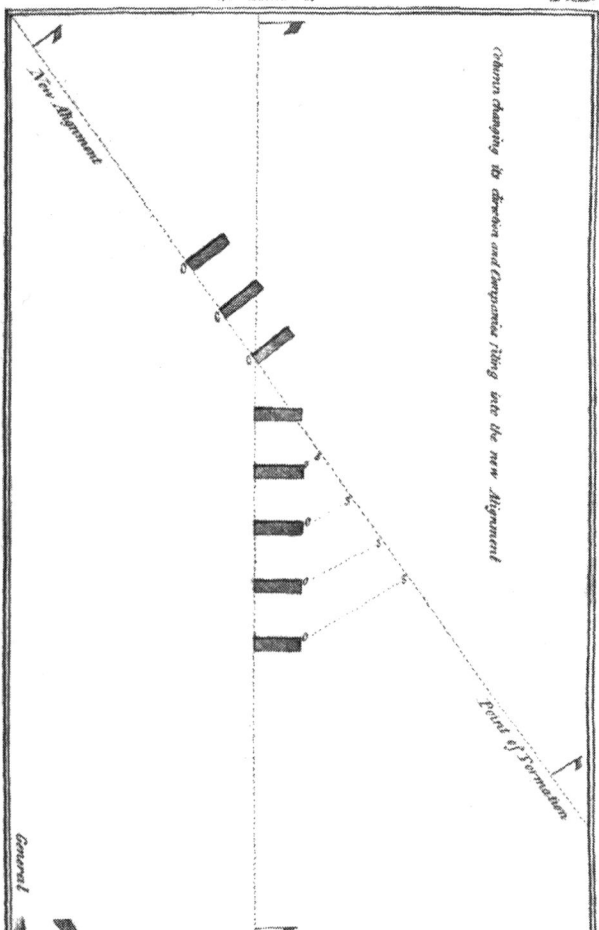

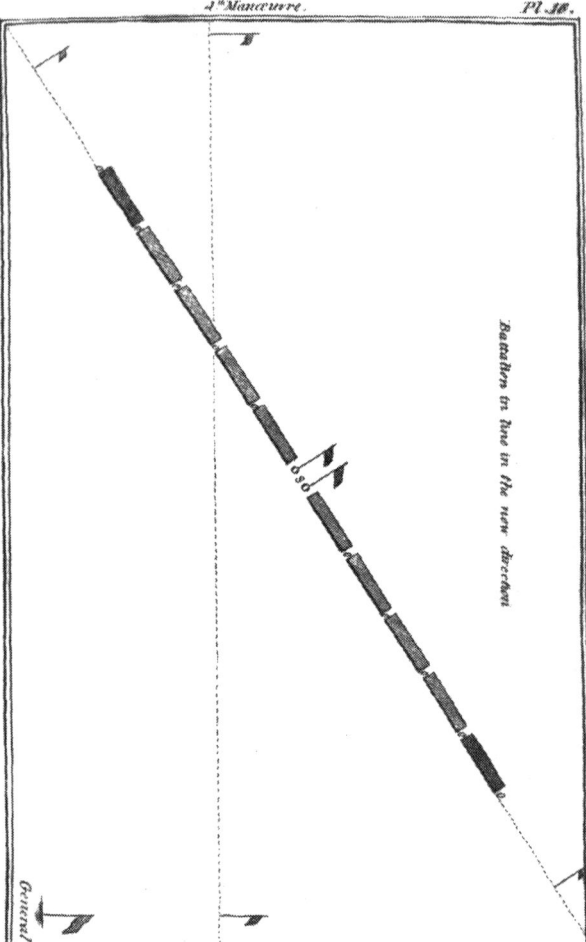

in *column*, and must always be well closed up before it deploys.

Rear ranks are one foot asunder.

Divisions are one pace asunder.

Officers and covering serjeants, are on the pivot-flanks of their companies.

The *left* when the right is in front.

The *right* when the left is in front.

Colours, supernumerary officers and serjeants, are on the reverse flank.

The colonel is in the front of the column, and places himself before the officer of the leading company, and from thence judging the perpendicular of the column, will attend to the officers covering each other in that direction as they come up.

The rest of the mounted officers, music, drummers and pioneers are in the rear of the column.

Artillery is either in the front, or on the reverse flank of the column when in march.

Fourth Manoeuvre.

(Plates 15 & 16.)

Change of Position in open Column.

WHEEL back into open column of companies, the right in front.

March forward 30 or 40 paces.

Enter an oblique line, the 3d or 4th leading companies,

panies, by wheeling succeffively to the left, a half wheel, halt.

The rear companies file into column.

Wheel up into line.

The battalion thus, at an intermediate point, enters an alignment, on which it is to form.

It is performed in the following manner:

The commanding officer gives the

CAUTION.

Companies to the left backwards Wheel.

Left-hand men of companies face inwards to their companies.

Officers ftep nimbly to the front of their companies, the ferjeant of the right-company fteps back, and remains to mark the fpot where the wheeling man of his company is to reft, when the quarter circle is completed: the other companies conform to this, each company ftanding perpendicular to the bafe line on which its pivot is placed.

Quick—*March.*

All the companies wheel back the quarter-circle on the principle already laid down.

Officers *Halt-Drefs* their companies, and then giving the words, *Eyes-Front,* remain on the pivot flank of their companies.

The battalion is now in open column of companies, the right in front.

The

The commanding officer gives the words—

COLUMN—*March.*

When the column has marched in ordinary time 30 or 40 paces, then the commanding officer gives the

CAUTION.

THE COLUMN WILL CHANGE ITS DIRECTION TO

THE LEFT.

The adjutant places two camp colours in an oblique direction to that line on which the column is moving to, the left of the pivot flank of the column. One colour is placed close to the pivot flank of the grenadiers, or leading company, where the new direction is to be taken, the other colour is placed considerably more to the left oblique, to where the line is to be formed, and a third colour is placed a distance in the rear, in line with the other. When the leading company comes near the first colour, it makes a half wheel on a moveable pivot, by its own officer giving the word—*Right Shoulders-Forward*—he keeps his eye fixed on the distant camp colour to which he steadily marches.

Each company, as it comes near the first colour, exactly conforms to what has been done by the leading company, on the principle of the moveable pivot; when the commanding officer sees as many companies
wheeled

wheeled into the new alignment as he judges sufficient, generally three, he then gives the words—

Column,

Halt.

He then gives the

Caution.

The rear Companies will file into the new

Alignment.

Rear Companies,

Right—*Face*.

The rear companies, that is, all the companies that have not made the half wheel into the new alignment, immediately face to the right, the officers move to the heads of files.

The covering serjeants of all the rear companies, step briskly on to mark the new alignment, where the left flank of their several companies are to be placed, —they take up their distances from the rear of the pivot-flank of the company, which last arrived in the new direction, and cover the pivots correctly.

Quick—*March*.

Each company moves to its covering serjeant, where its officer halts, and the company passes in rear of the
serjeant,

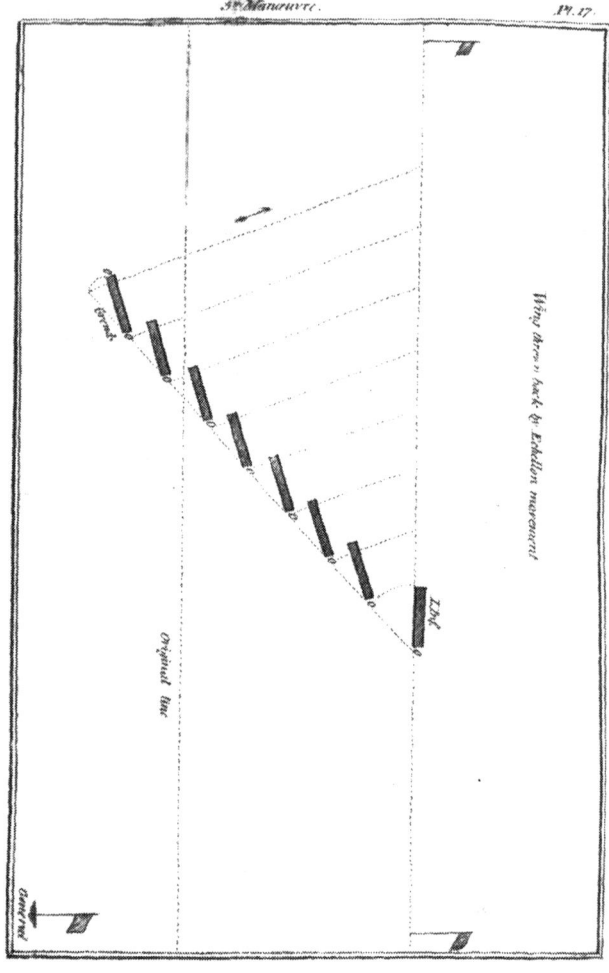

serjeant, till its left flank is in with him. He then gives the words, *Halt-Front, Dress.*

The commanding officer then gives the

Caution.

Column,

To the Left wheel into Line,

Quick--*March.*

The serjeant of the grenadiers moves quickly to the right, and places himself in line with the pivots; the rest of the covering serjeants go as usual to their right flanks to keep the place for their officers. When the wheel is completed, the company officers give the words, *Halt-Dress,* from the third file on their right, to the camp colour on their left, and immediately replace their covering serjeants.

Fifth Manoeuvre.

Wing thrown back.

THE left company is wheeled back, till parallel to the original position.

The rest of the companies wheel into Echellon*. March to the rear.—Form on the left company.

---

* *From Echelle, a ladder, is formed from line by the wheel of divisions less than the quarter-circle, the divisions are placed like a flight of steps, or organ pipes. The divisions are not placed behind each other, but are parallel to each other in the Echellon coloumn. The attacks of considerable bodies are almost always conducted on the principles of the Echellon.*

The whole companies wheel back at the same time; the left company twice the number of paces that the others do,

Should it be necessary for the subsequent movements, the line may retire 50 or 60 paces, and then front.

It is performed in the following manner:

The commanding officer gives the

CAUTION.

The left, or light infantry company, will wheel four paces backwards on its left; the remaining companies will go to the right about and wheel two paces to their right,—or, they may, if so ordered, wheel backward into Echellon.

The covering serjeant of the left company now steps to the rear, and on the 8th file from the pivot, marches the named number of paces, and comes to the right about, lining himself with the camp colour, placed by the adjutant on the right, to mark the new line, which is to be parallel to the original line of formation.

The commanding officer then gives the

CAUTION.

LEFT COMPANY,

FOUR PACES ON YOUR LEFT BABKWARDS WHEEL.

QUICK—*March.*

The

The ferjeant halts the company, and the officer accurately dreffes it on the colour to the right.

Remaining Companies—right about

Face.

They go to the right about.

Companies,

Two Paces to the right wheel,

March.

Each covering ferjeant fteps out, and marks the diftance, that is, two paces, or a 16th of the circle, he halts the company, and his officer dreffes it.

The battalion now ftands in Echellon, with its rear ranks in front, the officers have fhifted to the inner flank of their feveral companies.

The Battalion will march in Echellion, and form Line on the left Company,

March.

The officer commanding the company next to the ftanding one, lets his company march on a full pace beyond it, places himfelf on the third file, on the right of the ftanding company, ann then gives his company the words, *Halt-Front, Drefs-up*—he accurately dreffes them on the camp colour on the right, then gives the word,

word, *Eyes-Front*, and places himself on the right of his company; every other company does the same till the line is formed, it is then parallel to its original line of formation, but more retired by the length of five companies, supposing the battalion consisted but of eight, and that three wheeled into the oblique alignment. The battalion is to the general's left.

N. B. To follow the plan as laid down in the last plate of the Rules and regulations, the battalion should now go to the right about, retire 50 or 60 paces, and then halt-front.

Sixth Manoeuvre.

Countermarch and Change of Position.

WHEEL back into open column, the right in front. Countermarch companies by files.

March in column 30 or 40 paces.—Head division halts close to the head of column.

Form solid square and prepare for firing, re-form in close column.

Open out to open column from the rear, and halt.

Change head of column by the countermarch of companies, from the rear to the front.—Column moves on and halts.—Wheel up into line.

After the countermarch by files, the column stands with its left in front.—The column closes in quick time.—The square is formed, and close column reformed.

6.th Manœuvre.   Pl. 10.

Column halted and opened from the center to form solid square

Solid Square preparatory to firing

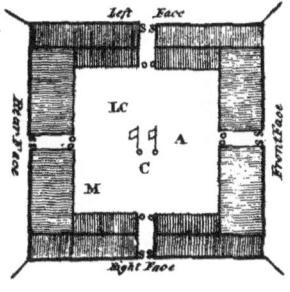

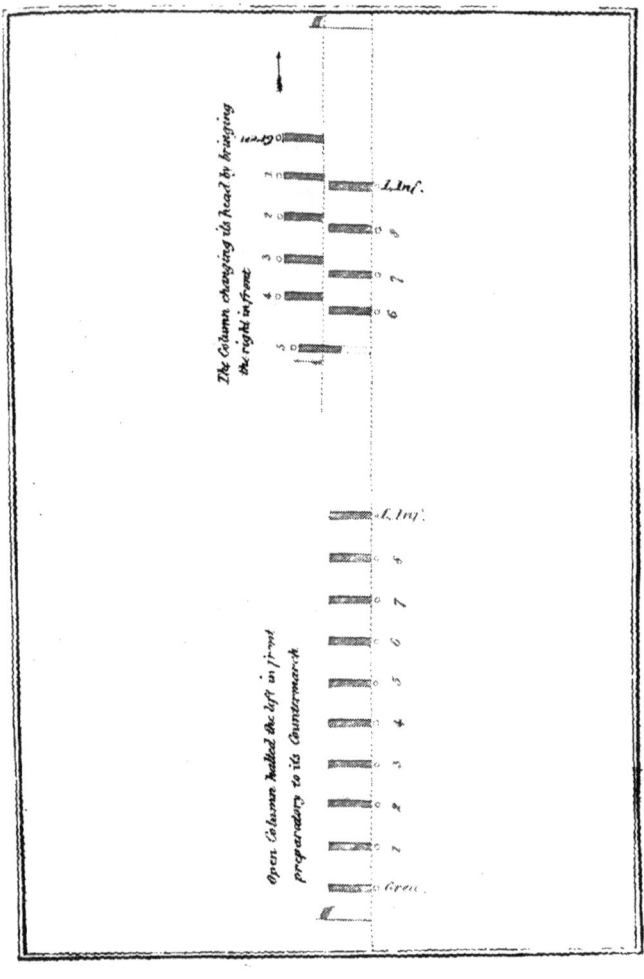

formed.—The column opens out in quick time from its rear division and halts.—The countermarch of companies from the rear to the front, is in ordinary time.—When the line is formed, it is then to the general's right and with its rear to him.

The whole is performed in the following manner:

The commanding officer gives the

CAUTION.

COMPANIES ON THE LEFT BACKWARDS WHEEL.

QUICK—*March.*

The battalion breaks into open column of companies, the right in front.

CAUTION.

COLUMN WILL CHANGE ITS FRONT BY THE COUNTERMARCH OF COMPANIES TO THE RIGHT.

COMPANIES,

RIGHT—*Face.*

At this word, the whole face to the right, each company officer will immediately quit the pivot, and place himself on the right of his company, and his covering serjeant will advance to the spot which he has quitted, and face to the right about.

RIGHT COUNTERMARCH.

QUICK

Quick—*March*.

At the word MARCH, the whole move, the officer wheels short round to the right, and proceeds, followed by his files of men, till he has placed his pivot front rank man close to his serjeant, who remains immovable. Each officer instantly gives the word, *Halt-Front, Dress*, to his company, so as to have it square, and closed to the right, which is now the pivot flank, and on which the officer now replaces his serjeant, who falls back behind the rear rank. The column at present stands faced to its former rear, with the left in front.

The commanding officer then gives the command,

Column—*March*.

The column marches 30 or 40 paces.

COLUMN WILL CLOSE TO THE FRONT.

The leading company immediately halts, and the remaining companies each halt within one pace of the company in its front.

Officers must be very careful to *halt-dress* their companies correctly, as this is preparatory to forming the solid square.

Observe—That the column may be closed at the option of the commander, either in this manner, or by the head division continuing its march, and the

rear

rear ones being ordered to MARCH QUICK into close column, and succeffively to refume the ordinary march.

The commanding officer then gives the words—

FORM SOLID SQUARE.

All the companies compofing the front half of the column, *i. e.* the left wing, take one pace forward, except the light-infantry, which ftands faft.

The two laft companies, clofe up one and two paces to the company before them.

Then the commanding officer gives the words—

SUB-DIVISIONS,

ONE PACE TO THE RIGHT AND LEFT,

March.

The whole companies make an interval of two paces in their centre, by their fubdivifions taking each one pace to the flanks.

Two officers with their ferjeants, place themfelves on each of the front and rear intervals, two officers with their ferjeants, alfo take poft in each of the increafed intervals in the centre of the fides; and a ferjeant *takes the place* of each flank front rank man of the firft divifion, and of each flank rear rank man of

the

the laſt diviſion; all the other officers, ſerjeants, the 4 diſplaced men, drummers, &c. aſſemble behind the centre of the companies which are to form the *flank faces*.

Four Files.

Outwards—*Face*.

The two rear ranks face to the right about, and four files, ſuppoſing the companies of 12 files each, on each flank of all the companies, except the grenadiers and light-infantry, face outwards, the whole lining with the flanks of the front companies, and dreſſing in ranks from front to rear.

Quick—*March*.

The 5th file from each flank of all the companies, except the two firſt and two laſt, followed by the front rank man of the 6th file, move up to right and left, and reſpectively fill up the interval between their own and the preceding diviſion ; the remainder of the men of the ſide diviſions, arrange themſelves to their right and left, forming cloſe in the rear of their own diviſions reſpectively.

The whole thus ſtand faced outwards, and formed at leaſt 4 deep, with 2 officers and their ſerjeants in the middle of each face to command.

The officers commanding companies may fill the intervals as follows :

The

Quick—*March.*

The front company takes one pace forward, and the two rear companies, that is, the grenadiers and firſt company, one and two paces forward, and then face about. The files from the intervals take their proper places, officers, ſerjeants, diſplaced men, &c. will quit the interior, move to their ſeveral ſtations, and the companies that compoſed the flank faces, will be completed.

Not to multiply words of command, the beſt method to cloſe the ſub diviſions, &c. is to move the column immediately, by giving the word

Column—*March,*

Either in quick or ordinary time, as the commanding officer ſees proper.

When the column has marched as far as the commandant judges proper, he gives the words—

Column will open from the Rear.

The officer commanding the rear company, immediately gives the word to his company, Grenadiers, *Halt,* and immediately gives the caution to the company in his front—first company—and when he ſees it exactly at a proper wheeling diſtance from him, he gives the word, *Halt*—the officer commanding the
firſt

first company, when he has halted gives the same caution and command to the second, the second to the third, &c. and so on in succession, till the column is opened out.

The commanding officer now gives the

CAUTION,

THE COLUMN WILL CHANGE ITS HEAD BY THE
COUNTERMARCH OF COMPANIES
FROM THE REAR.

RIGHT WING.—*To the Front.*

The grenadier officer gives the word, GRENADIERS, *Left-Face*—he, and his covering serjeant immediately shift to the left to lead the files—*Quick-March*, till his *right* flank can freely pass near the *left* flank of the others; he then gives the words—*Halt-Front-March,* close by the right flank of the company then preceding him: the officer commanding that company, as soon as the other approaches him, orders, COMPANY, *Left-Face, Quick-March,* behind the now leading one, *Halt-Front,* when he covers, and then *March,* when at the due wheeling distance. All the other companies successively perform the same operation; and when the light-company has taken its place in the rear, the whole column is in perfect order, with its right in front.

COLUMN-

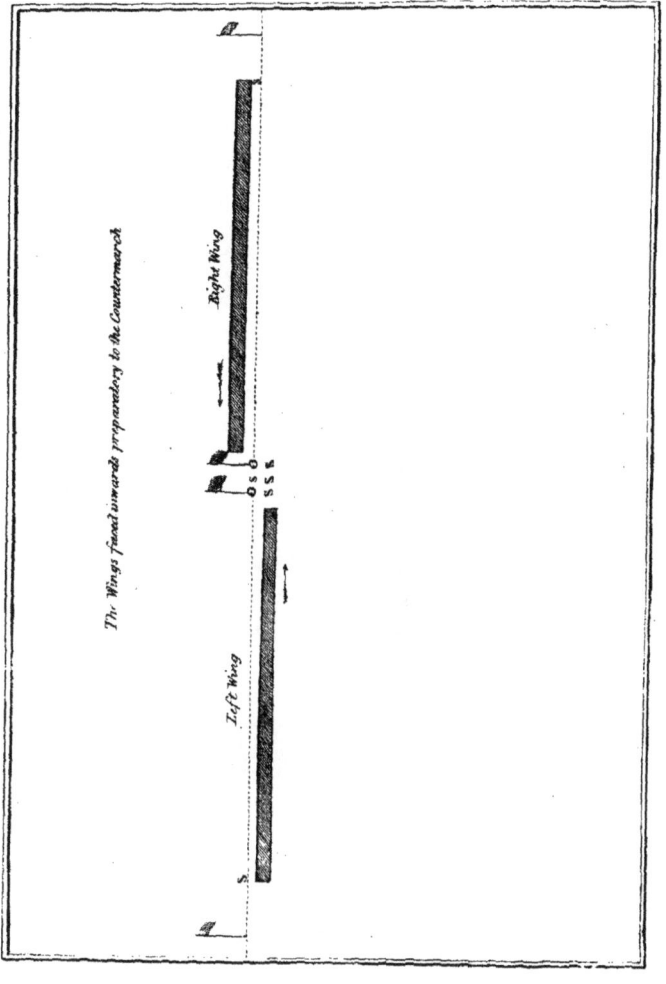

Pl. 21

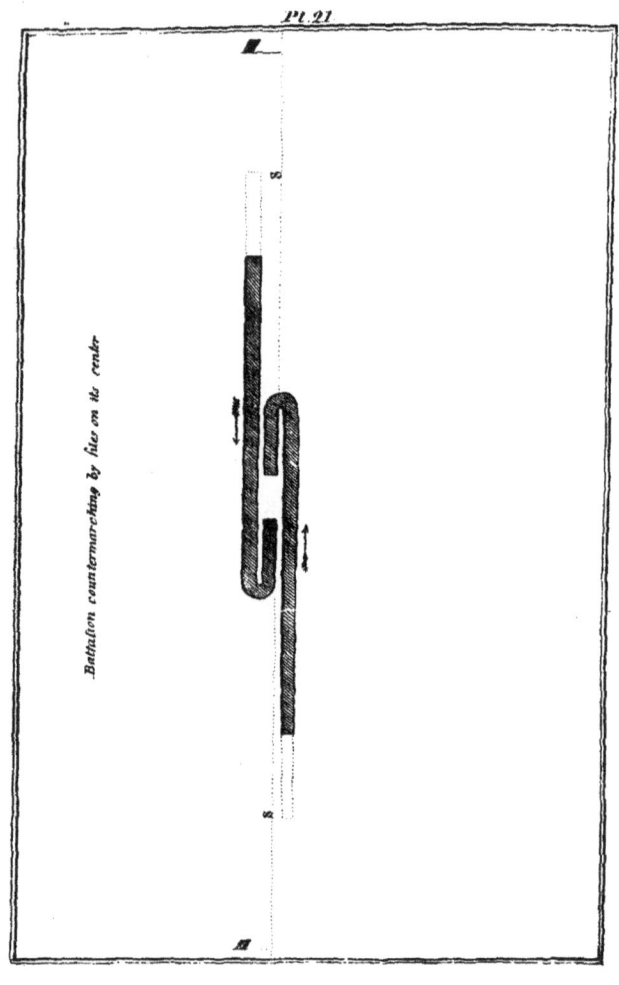

Battalion countermarching by files on the center

Column—*Halt.*

Companies to the Left wheel into Line.

Quick—*March.*

The battalion is now in line, considerably to the general's right, and with its rear to him.

Observe—That some regiments at review, in the countermarch from the rear to the front, face their companies to the *right*, and bring them out on that side, contrary to the *general principle*, that the divisions which advance come out always on the side to which front is to be made, and on which the enemy, is placed, because then with the divisions which are free, he can be opposed, while the others are moving behind the line.

Seventh Manoeuvre.

Countermarch by Files on the Centre of the Battalion.

THIS brings back the battalion to its original front.

The commanding officer gives the

Caution,

The

THE BATTALION WILL COUNTERMARCH FROM ITS
CENTRE, AND ON ITS CENTRE BY FILES.

WINGS,

INWARDS—*Face*.

The whole face to the colours, which stand fast, and a serjeant remains to mark each flank of the battalion

WINGS.

THREE SIDE STEPS TO THE RIGHT.

If the battalion is two deep, 2 paces to the right is sufficient.

March.

Each wing takes the named number of paces to its right, that they may be disengaged from each other.

March.

At this second word march, or *quick-march*, the whole move on, and each file wheels successively into the centre as it arrives at, and beyond the colours. As soon as each company is in the line from the colours to the flank serjeant, its officer *fronts* it. When the whole is formed, the colours countermarch, and the

8th Manœuvre.   Pl. 22.

Forming open Column of Comp.s in rear of the Light Infantry

Grend, 1, 2, 3, 4, 5, 6, L.t Inf.

Grend, 1, 2, 3, 4, 5, 6, L.t Inf.

Column of Sub divisions

General

the whole are looking to the colours till otherwise ordered.

Eighth Manoeuvre.

March in open Column.

FORM open column behind the left company, which is put in march when the 3d company has taken its place in column.

The right sub-divisions double.

The right sub-divisions move up.

The column halts, and pivots are corrected. Wheel up into line.

The companies that are filing incline towards the head of the column: successively front at their wheeling distances, ascertained as usual by their serjeants; take up the ordinary step, and follow in open column.

When the column is marching steadily, the whole sub-divisions double at once by one command, and again move up at another.

It is performed in the following manner:

The commanding officer gives the

Caution,

The

The Battalion will form open Column in rear of the left Company, or Light Infantry.

Remaining Companies,

On the Right backward Wheel,

Quick—*March.*

All the companies wheel backward on their right, except the left company, which stands fast.

Left—*Face.*

All the companies will face to the left, except the light company, and the officers place themselves to lead.

Quick—*March.*

At the word march, the whole will lead to the rear, and the covering serjeants will succeffively, as before, take up their pivot points on the new line.— The officer conducting each platoon, when he arrives at his serjeant, will stop directly before him, allow his platoon to move on behind the serjeant, till the rear file comes close to, but beyond him; the officer will then *halt-front, dress* his platoon to the right,

per-

perpendicular to the new direction, and with his front rank closed into the serjeant.

As soon as the 3d company has taken its place in the column,

The commanding officer gives the word to the column,

March.

The head of it moves on in *ordinary time*, and the remaining companies follow, preserving the proper wheeling distance between each. When the leading company arrives within 12 or 15 paces of the point where it is necessary to diminish its front, the commander will give a loud CAUTION, that the subdivisions are to double either by companies successively, or the whole battalion at once—*if at once*, as is ordered in this manœuvre, then he gives the words—

FORM COLUMN OF SUB DIVISION.

RIGHT SUB-DIVISIONS,

Mark Time.

The right-hand sub-divisions mark time, till its left-hand sub-division, which marches on steadily, has opened or cleared its flank.

QUICK—

Quick—*Oblique;* or left oblique.

The right divisions immediately oblique to the left, and cover the left correctly.

The officers commanding companies move to the right flank of the left sub-divisions, their covering serjeants lead the right sub-division.

It may be observed, that the above is in conformity to the *general rule*, whether the column be halted or in motion, *that the sub-division or section on the reverse flank, is the one behind which the other sub-division, or section, doubles.* But in this case, were the left sub-divisions to double in front of the right ones, the pivots would be better dressed, as the right sub-divisions which were marching correctly in the alignment would not be discomposed.

When the open column of sub divisions has marched as many paces as the commanding officer sees proper, he again forms them into companies.

Form Companies.

Right Sub-divisions,

Quick—*Oblique.*

As soon as the right sub-divisions clear the right flank of the left sub-divisions, **by** the quick oblique, they

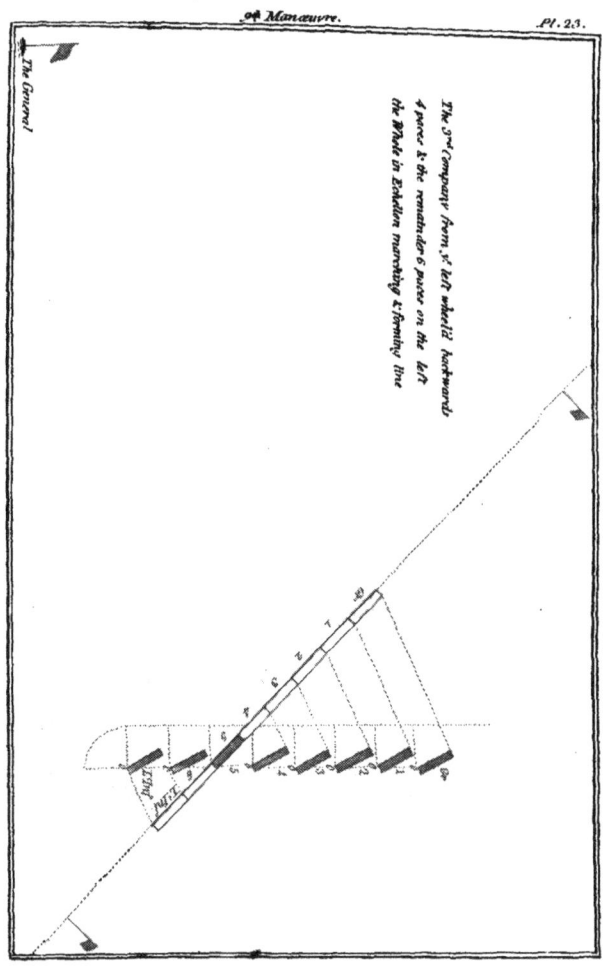

they immediately receive the word *forward*, and when they get up in line with the left sub-divisions, they receive the word *ordinary* from the commander of the company, who had shifted to its right.

COLUMN.

Halt.

TO THE LEFT WHEEL INTO LINE.

QUICK—*March.*

NINTH MANOEUVRE.

ECHELLON CHANGE OF POSITION.

WHEEL back into open column, the left in front.

The 3d company from the left is wheeled back, the 8th of the circle, and each of the others 3-16ths of the circle.

Form line on the 3d company by the Echellon march.

The line is thus formed oblique from open column, on a central company by the Echellon march, in the following manner:

The commanding officer gives the words,

COMPANIES

Companies on the Right,

Backwards—*Wheel.*

Quick—*March.*

The battalion breaks into open column, the left in front, each company gets the word, *Halt-Dress* from its own officer as usual.

The colonel gives the

Caution,

The third Company will Wheel four Paces, the Remaining Companies two Paces on the Left backwards.

Quick—*March.*

The companies are dressed by their officers, who are now on the inside flanks of the Echellon, a serjeant is on each outside or reverse flank.

Eighth and Light Companies,

Right about—*Face.*

Two camp colours are sent to the right and left in a correct line with the 3d company.

The colonel then gives the

Caution,

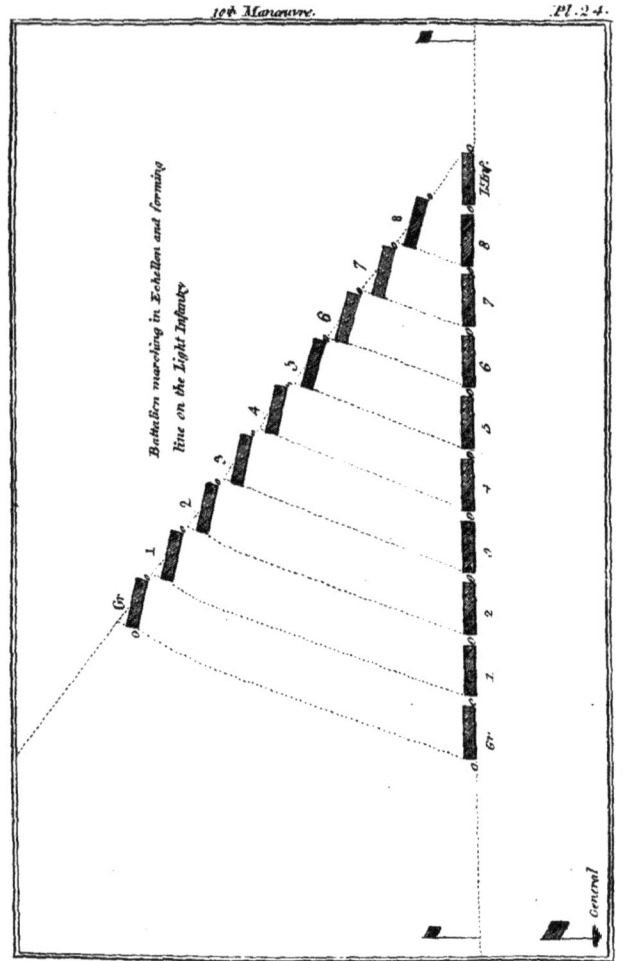

Caution,

Column will March in Echellon, and form Line on the third Company.

March.

The officer of the 3d company shifts to its right flank.

Each company on the right of the 3d, as it comes succesively into line, receives from its own officer the words *halt-dress*, on the camp colour to the right, the officer then shifts to the right of his company; the companies on the left of the 3d company, receive the words from their officers, *Halt-Front*, *Dress up*, they are dressed on the camp colour to the left, on the principle of the 3d manoeuvre.

Tenth Manoeuvre.

Echellon change of Position.

THE left company is wheeled up the 8th of the circle, and each of the others 1-16th. Form line by the Echellon march.

The line thus changes position to the front on the left company, by the Echellon march.

The colonel gives the

Caution,

CAUTION,

THE LIGHT-INFANTRY WILL WHEEL FOUR PACES,
THE REMAINING COMPANIES TWO PACES
TO THE LEFT.

Covering ferjeants take the named number of paces from the front of the 8th file from the left of their companies; the left-hand man of the front rank of the light-infantry company makes a half pace, and thofe of the remaining companies a quarter face to the left, dreffing by the covering ferjeants.

The colonel gives the word

QUICK—*March*.

The officer commanding the light company immediately fhifts to its left flank; when the company has wheeled up, he gives the word *halt-drefs*, drefling it correctly on the camp colour which the adjutant had previoufly fent to the right for this purpofe; the officer, when his company is correctly dreffed, gives the word *Eyes-Front*, and refumes his place on the right of his company, taking care that his men ftand perfectly fteady and with carried arms, until the next company has dreffed on their right flank, being their *Appui*.

When the commanding officer fees that every divifion is ready, he gives the

CAUTION,

(99)

Caution.

The Battalion will march in Echelon, and form Line on the left Company.

March.

All the companies march in ordinary time; as they arrive in line succeſsively, they are dreſſed by their own officers from the ſtanding companies to the camp colour on the right; each officer, when he has ſo dreſſed his company, gives the word *Eyes-Front*, and ſhifts to the right of his company.

The whole are now formed in line, parallel to the original front, and conſiderably to the general's right.

Eleventh Manoeuvre.

Change of Position.

THE battalion faces to the right.

Marches in file 50 or 60 paces.

Forms column of companies on the march.—Halts. —Wheels up into line, if the light-company is to manœuvre, it files quickly to the right, and forms behind the colours.

The column of companies is formed by the rear men of each moving up quick to the left of their leaders, and of each other: the officers move to pivot flanks, and pivots are inſtantly corrected. The column halts when the colours are oppoſite to the general.

The colonel gives the

Caution.

Caution.

The Battalion will form open Column of Companies on the March.

Right—*Face.*

March.

When the battalion has marched in files as far as the commander judges neceſſary, he gives the word

Form—*Companies.*

The files inſtantly make a half-face, each marching up quick and *diagonally* to their reſpective leading men, who do not alter their pace: as the pivots are in the rear of companies, when they do come up, the companies dreſs to them by their officer giving the word, *Eyes-Left*—and they take up as they form the ordinary ſtep.

When the colours are oppoſite to the general,

Column—*Halt.*

To the Left—Wheel into Line.

Quick—*March.*

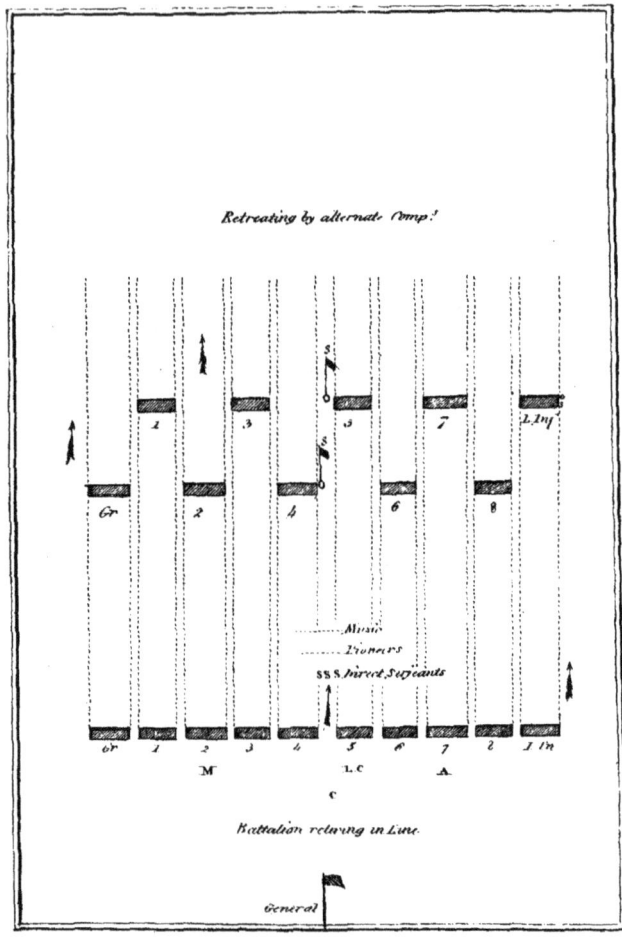

Twelfth Manoeuvre.

Retreat in Line.

THE battalion retires 50 paces, halts, fronts, Fires, twice by companies from centre to flanks.

Retire by alternate companies in two lines, 250 paces, each retreat about 50 paces.

Retire in line 50 paces, halt, front.

The light company being previously sub-divided and prepared, acts in the retreat by alternate companies, and when the line halts and fronts, it resumes its place on the left *.

The colonel gives the

Caution.

The Battalion will Retire,

Right about Face,

March.

It marches 50 or 60 paces in ordinary time, dressing by its centre.

Halt—*Front.*

Caution.

The Battalion will Fire twice by Companies from Centre to Flanks.

On

---

* *There being no light company in the 1st Regiment of R. E. V. this is of course omitted.*

On the last stroke of the preparative, the officers on the right of companies step out one pace, and give the word of command—*Company, Ready, Pfent, Fire, Load.* When the first part of the general is beat, the officers fall back into the front rank.

The colonel gives the

CAUTION.

THE BATTALION WILL RETIRE BY ALTERNATE COMPANIES.

RIGHT COMPANIES,

RIGHT ABOUT—*Face.*

March.

The right companies march in ordinary time about 50 paces, when they receive the words,

HALT—*Front.*

In marching, one colour remains on the flank of its proper company in each line, and directs its movements, for which purpose, a serjeant will advance 6 paces before it during the march.—Distances are preserved from that colour.—The eyes of each line remain turned to their colour.

Each line has a command.—Officers are ordered to be on the inward flanks of their companies—but this
makes

makes a perpetual shifting of positions, and is generally omitted.

The colonel gives the word

LEFT COMPANIES,

MAKE READY-PRESENT—*Fire.*

Immediately after firing, the men come to the recover, half cock, and shoulder arms.

The colonel gives the word,

RIGHT ABOUT—*Face.*

March.

The left companies march steadily on, dressing by their colour, they pass through the intervals of the right companies, and continue marching until they receive the word from the commanding officer.

HALT—*Front.*

PRIME AND *Load.*

If the colonel fires the left companies the lieutenant colonel then fires the right companies exactly as the left companies were fired; they retire in the same manner, through the intervals of the left companies.

The colonel then fires the left companies and retires them as before, and so on till he thinks it expedient to form line, hethen gives the.

CAUTION.

Caution.

The Left-companies
Will form Line on the Right Companies,

March.

When they have marched and filled up the intervals, he gives the word,

Halt,

And the officer of each company gives the word,

Drefs.

The right companies may form line on the left in the fame manner. Sometimes the right companies are fired in battalion, previous to their retiring; the words of command are the fame as if they had been feparated from the left companies.

The light infantry may be divided in the intervals of the firft line, retire with it, and change to the other line whenever it becomes the advanced one; in this fituation they cover the retreat, and may occafionally fire; and when the line is formed, they refume their poft on the left.

Unlefs the battalion is very ftrong, the light-infantry remain in their ufual pofition.

When the line is formed, the colonel gives the
Caution.

CAUTION.

THE BATTALION WILL RETIRE IN LINE,

RIGHT-ABOUT—*Face.*

March—Halt—Front.

THIRTEENTH MANOEUVRE.

MARCH TO A FLANK IN ECHELLON.

COMPANIES make a half wheel to the right.
March in Echellon 250 paces.

Wheel back on the march into parallel line—Forward 100 paces, halt.

Fire thrice by companies from flanks to centre.

At the word, wheel back into line, the pivot flanks mark time, and the division wheel back in ordinary time. At the proper instant when the battalion is formed, the commander gives his word forward, for the whole to advance by the colours, and to correct any irregularity that there may be in the battalion.

CAUTION.

BATTALION—BY COMPANIES, FOUR PACES TO THE RIGHT-WHEEL, AND FORM ECHELLON.

Covering

Covering serjeants take the named number of paces as usual from the 8th file from the right, the pivots make a half-face to the right, the serjeants dressing by them.

Quick—*March.*

Officers on the right give the words, *Halt-Dress*; covering serjeants go to the reverse flank.

Commanding officer then gives the

Caution.

The Battalion will advance in Echellon,

March.

The whole advance in Echellon about 250 paces.

Wheel back into Line.

The three centre serjeants instantly step out into the front and mark the time.

The pivots mark time, gradually turning to their proper front, while the rest of the division wheel back the 4 paces they had advanced; when the 4th pace is completed, the line should get the word

Forward.

The whole dressing by the centre, step out their full pace.

Halt.

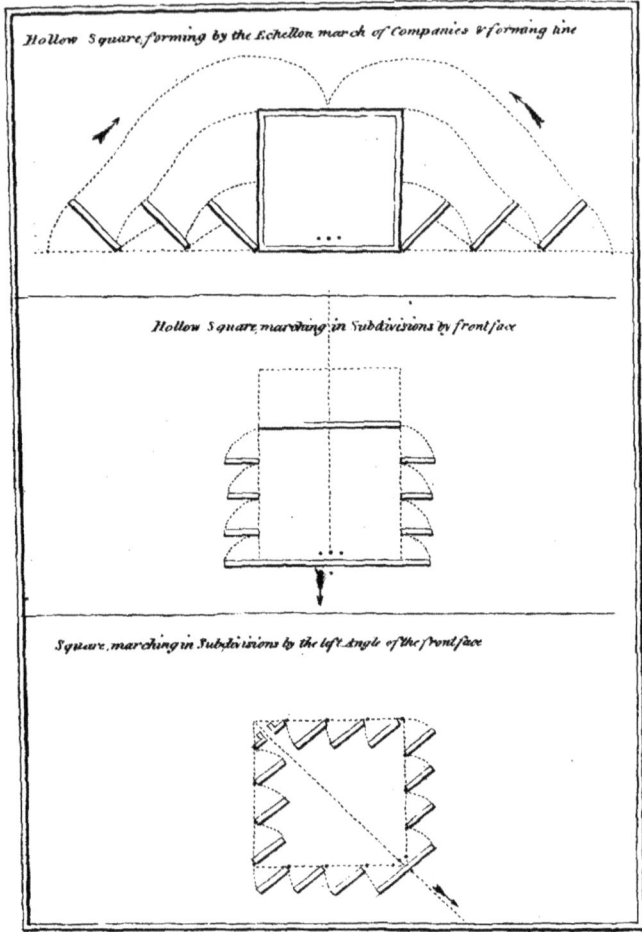

Halt.

Fire three rounds by companies from centre to flanks.

The line is considerably to the general's left, parallel to its original front.

Fourteenth Manoeuvre.

Hollow Square and its Movements.

FORM square.

March the square by the left angle of the front face 50 paces, Halt, Form Square.

March square by the left face, Halt, Form Square.

March square by the rear face, 60 paces, halt, form square.

Fire in square by companies.

Form the line.

The square is formed by the Echellon march of companies.

After the march by the left face, the square is formed when it is oppofite the general.

The line is formed by the Echellon wheel up, and march of companies.

When the order is given to form line, the light-company, if it acts feparately, marches quickly, and

places

places itself two deep, and in two divisions, 10 or 11 paces behind the two centre companies.

The whole is performed in the following manner, with 8 companies.

The colonel gives the

CAUTION,

THE BATTALION WILL FORM A HOLLOW SQUARE ON THE TWO CENTRE COMPANIES.

REMAINING COMPANIES,

FOUR PACES ON THE RIGHT AND LEFT BACKWARD-WHEEL,

QUICK—*March*.

The three companies on the right, each wheel back the 8th of the circle on their left, the three companies on the left, wheel the same number of paces backwards on their right.

The colours at the same time that the companies are forming their Echellons, move back three paces into the rear, the 4th company by the side-step inclines to the 5th company, to close the interval that was made by the falling back of the colours.

RIGHT-ABOUT—*Face*.

The companies that were in Echellon, face to the right about.

The colonel then gives the

CAUTION.

IN ECHELLON MARCH TO FORM SQUARE,

March.

Two serjeants or camp colours, should be placed in the rear in a perpendicular line with the outside flanks of the front face, marking out a perfect square; the companies now march in Echellon, and by the turning of the left shoulders of the right companies, and the right shoulders of the left companies, they wheel in to form square, their officers halt and front them in a correct line, the grenadiers will wheel round the serjeant placed to mark the angle, the light-infantry at the same time wheeling round the serjeant on the opposite angles, till their two right flanks touch, when they get the words *halt-front, dress*, from their officers, and have then formed the *rear* face of the square, and in this manner will the proper front rank of the rear face be outward. The square is perfectly formed, and composed of four faces: the front face consists of the 4th and 5th company, the right-face of the 3d and 2d, the left face of the 6th and 7th, and the rear-face of the 1st and 8th company, that is, the grenadier and light infantry.

The mounted officers, colours, music drummers, &c. and the battalion guns, are all within the square.

The colonel gives the

Caution.

The Square will march by the Left Angle of the front Face.

Right and rear faces, right about—*Face.*

The two *sides* that form the left angle, that is, the front face and the left face stand fast; the other two sides, that is, the right face and the rear face, go to the right-about.

By Sub-divisions to the Right and Left half-wheel,

March.

The whole then by sub-divisions wheel up 1-8th of the circle, two sides to the right, and two sides to the left, and are thus parallel to each other, and perpendicular to the direction in which they are to move, the pivot flanks being in this manner placed on the sides of the square. Each side being thus in Echellon, and the colours behind the leading angle, the square gets the word—

March.

Officers commanding companies on the inward flank of their leading sub-divisions, carefully preserv-

ing

ing the distances they wheeled at, and from the flanks to which they wheeled.

Halt.

Front—*Square*; or, Re-form—*Square*

The whole wheel back into square, and the two sides that require it, that is, the right and rear faces go to the right about. Officers of companies dress their divisions as usual, in the same manner as is described for the square.

The directions given for the march of the square by the left angle of the front face, will equally apply, should it be found necessary to march the square by any of its other angles.

The colonel then gives the

Caution,

The Square will march by the Right-face

The colours move up behind the centre of the named face, as do the mounted officers, &c. &c.

Front and rear Faces, by Sub-divisions to the Right and Left Wheel.

Quick—*March.*

The

The opposite side, that is the left face, faces about; and the two flank sides wheel up by sub-divisions, so as to stand each in open column.

By Right—Face.

March.

The square marches two sides in line, and by their centre; and two sides in open column, which cover and dress to their inward flanks on which they wheeled up, carefully preserving their distances.

The same directions that are given for marching by the right-face, will apply to the march by any of the other faces.

The colonel, when the square has marched as far as he sees necessary, gives the word

Halt.

Re-form—*Square.*

Ths square halts, the sub-divisions in column immediately wheel back, and form their sides, and the side which faced about again faces outwards. Officers of companies give the words, *Halt-Dress.*

The colonel gives the

Caution,

Prepare for Firing.

The front rank kneels, and prefent their bayonets floped.

The fquare is then ordered to fire in whatever manner the colonel may judge proper; the two rear ranks to fire ftanding: or companies by ranks fucceffively, or by companies, independent of each other, by fubdivifions, one firing when the other has loaded: or companies by files, as ordered; the front rank remaining as a referve: fhould the battalion be formed only two deep, the front rank will remain kneeling, and the other rank will fire by files.

The Colonel orders,

SQUARE WILL FIRE BY COMPANIES, BEGINNING ON THE RIGHT.

When the firing by companies has ceafed,

The command is given by the colonel,

KNEELING RANKS,

MAKE READY—*Prefent-Fire.*

The men rifing up after firing,

Prime and Load.

The colonel gives the

CAUTION,

THE SQUARE WILL FORM LINE ON THE TWO CENTRE COMPANIES.

SIDE AND REAR FACES, BY COMPANIES, SIX PACES TO THE RIGHT AND LEFT WHEEL,

QUICK—*March.*

Officers HALT-DRESS their companies.

IN ECHELLON MARCH AND FORM LINE,

March.

 The whole march in Echellon, except the two centre companies, the outward companies taking care not to impede the inner ones, which muſt form before them; this may be done by the facing and filing of each diviſion from its inward flank, to its point in the new line where it will form up. Officers *Halt-Dreſs* their companies as in the third manœuvre.
 If the ſquare is compoſed of the eight battalion companies only, then the grenadier and light compa-

ny

ny may be placed as a reserve in the rear, ready to be applied according to circumstances *.

Fifteenth Maneouvre.

Retiring and filing to the Rear.

RETIRE in line 100 paces.
File by companies from the proper right.
Halt in open column, the right in front.
Wheel up into line.

When the line has passed the light company 20 paces, that company extends to cover the centre of the battalion, and follows at 50 or 60 paces distance; and when the column halts to form, the light company passes quickly through and beyond it.

The companies file quick to the rear.

The battalion forms line at the extremity of its ground, the light company 30 paces in its rear.

When the battalion is to retire, it ought to be previously dressed with the same exactness as when it was to ad-

---

* *In marching the square by any of its faces, instead of wheeling out the other two sides in open column of sub-divisions, if the men march tolerably in file, there can be no question, but that it is the best method; it is done in a moment, at the word,* SQUARE, WILL MARCH BY THE RIGHT—*Face.*

No other word is given, the front face, instantly faces to the right, the rear face to the left, the left face of the square comes to the right-about; at the word March, *the whole move, at the word* HALT, *the whole face outwards at once.*

advance, and the same care in ascertaining the direction of its march must be taken; therefore, before the retreat is to begin, an officer or serjeant will have placed himself 30 paces in the rear, so as to stand perpendicular to the front directing serjeant, and of course he will be in the line, or nearly so, of the directing serjeant: whenever the battalion marches to the rear, it must cover its proper extent of ground. The rear must therefore avoid closing their files more then usual, otherwise the front rank men, who are in general larger, will be crowded in their rank. Music, drums, supernumerary officers, &c. will take care to march with exactness, not to interrupt, but rather to assist the battalion.

The colonel gives the

CAUTION,

THE BATTALION WILL RETIRE.

As soon as this caution is given, the three directing serjeants face about, the same centre serjeant that directs to the front, directs also to the rear; he moves on in the line of the advance officer six paces beyond the rear rank, and halts; and the other two serjeants are on each side of him.

When the line is retiring, music is never to play.

RIGHT ABOUT—*Face.*

The whole face, and the supernumerary officer who had replaced the directing serjeant, moves up into the leading rank: a mounted field-officer passes through to the rear, and the directing serjeant in the interior, prolongs his line, and takes his object betwixt the feet of the posted officer—*immediately* after facing about, the word is given,

March.

The whole battalion instantly step off, the replacing officer betwixt the colours, preserves, during the movement, his exact distance of six paces from the advance serjeant, and is the guide of the battalion, the directing serjeant conducting on his points under the correction of the commanding officer generally, who is 10 or 12 paces behind the battalion.

In this retreat, if the light-infantry act separately, and not as a part of the battalion, at the word *March*, they move quickly round by the flanks, and form in the rear of the centre, extending so as to cover it during the retreat, and following at the distance of 50 or 60 paces.

After the battalion has marched 100 paces,

It receives the

CAUTION,

THE BATTALION WILL FORM THE PROPER RIGHT OF COMPANIES, FILE TO THE REAR.

Pass

Pass Companies by Files.

Each company officer instantly gives the word LEFT-*Turn*, QUICK-*March*, and wheels out his leading file, the rest of the files following in succession. The heads of companies must observe the proper distance from each, and are regulated from the left.

Circumstances may require, that the companies should *pass* from their proper left, instead of the right, in which case the leaders will shift and conduct such left, until the line is formed, when they will again resume their proper places.

When the companies in file have marched as far as is necessary, the commanding officer gives the word,

HALT—*Front*.

The whole now stand in open column of companies, the right in front.

LEFT WHEEL INTO LINE,

QUICK—*March*.

Officers as usual, *Halt-Dress* their companies. When the column is ordered to *Halt*, the light-company passes quickly through it, and takes post 30 paces in the rear of the intended line.

Sixteenth Manoeuvre.

Filing, advancing, and changing to the Front.

ADVANCE in line 50 paces.

File from the right of companies to the front, 50 paces.

Halt in open column, the left in front.

Wheel up into line.

Advance in line 50 paces.

Advance by alternate half battalions, and fire four times.

Form line, advance 50 paces. Fire volley, advance 20 paces.

Charge bayonets 50 paces, Halt, Load.

Before the line advances, the light company quickly forms, extended 30 paces before the centre, and preserves that distance in advancing.

When the column halts to form, the light company passes quick to the rear, and assembles, half of it behind each flank, and moves relatively with the flank companies, till after the charge of bayonets.

The alternate half battalions fire, the two first ranks standing.

After the volley, bayonets are ported, the battalion advances firm by the centre at the quick step, and at the word *Halt*, the front rank comes down to the charging position.

The word Prime and Load is then given, and the light company iffuing from behind the flanks, purfue, return, and affemble and join on the flank of the battalion.

The commanding officer having previoufly placed himfelf 10 or 12 paces behind the exact line of the directing ferjeant, will remark the line of its prolongation, and thereby afcertain the direction in which it fhould march, and in doing this, he will not at once look out for a diftant object, but will hit on it, by prolonging the line from the perfon of the directing ferjeant to the front: or, he will order the covering ferjeant to run out 20 paces, and will place him in the line in which he thinks the battalion ought to advance. The directing ferjeant then takes his direction along the line which paffes from himfelf, betwixt the heels of the advanced ferjeant, and remarking his object preferves fuch line in advancing.

The colonel then gives the

Caution,

The Battalion will Advance.

On which the front directing ferjeant moves fix accurate and exact paces, in ordinary time, and halts; the two other ferjeants that were behind him move up on each fide of him, and an officer from the rear replaces in the front rank the leading ferjeant. The

center

centre serjeant in moving out, marches and halts on his own obferved point, and the other two ferjeants drefs and fquare themfelves exactly by him. The directing ferjeant, after being affured that he himfelf is perfectly and fquarely placed in the rank, by cafting his eyes down the centre of his body, from the junction of his two heels, and by repeated trials to take up prolong a line perpendicular to himfelf and to the battalion: then he will obferve, and take up any accidental fmall fpot on the ground, and within 100 or 150 paces, intermediate ones cannot be wanting, nor the renewal of fuch as he afterwards fucceffively approaches to in his march. In this manner he is prepared, under the future correction of the commanding officer from behind, to conduct the march.

The line of direction being thus afcertained, the colonel then gives the word

March.

The whole inftantly ftep off, and without turning the head, eyes are glanced towards the colours, in the front rank: the replacing officer betwixt the colours, preferves during the movement, his exact diftance of fix paces from the advanced ferjeant, and is the guide of the battalion. The centre advanced ferjeant is anfwerable for the direction, and the equal cadence and length of ftep: to thefe objects he alone attends, while the other two, fcrupuloufly conforming to his pofition, maintain their parallelifm to the front of the battalion,

talion, and thereby present an object to which it ought to move square: they are to allow no other considerations to distract their attention, and will notice and conform to the direction of the commander only; and if any small alteration in their position is ordered, it must be gradually and coolly made.

When the battalion is advancing in line for any considerable distance, the music may be allowed at intervals to play; for a *few seconds only*, and the drums in two divisions to roll; but it is the wind instruments only which play; the large drum, or any other instrument whatever, which marks time by the stroke, is not to be permitted.

When the battalion advances 50 paces,

The colonel gives the

CAUTION.

THE BATTALION WILL FILE FROM THE RIGHT OF

COMPANIES.

PASS—FILES—*to the Front*.

Each company officer immediately gives the word, RIGHT-*Turn*, QUICK-*March*; he wheels out his leading file and passes on to the front, preserving a relative distance from the left, as being the head of the column, or from the other flank, if particularly so ordered. When the column has marched 50 paces,

The colonel gives the word,

HALT—

Halt—*Front.*

The whole now stand in open column, the left in front—pivots are corrected. They then get the

Caution,

To the Right—*Wheel into Line,*

Quick—*March.*

Officers *Halt-Dress* their companies as usual.

The colonel then gives the

Caution.

The Battalion will Advance.

March.

The battalion marches 50 paces.

The colonel gives the

Caution.

The Battalion will Advance by alternate Wings, and fire four Times.

Observe—There must be a commander for each half battalion, or wing.

The colonel then gives the

Caution.

CAUTION.

LEFT-WING—*Halt.*

The Left Wing Halts, and the Right Wing continues to move on 15 paces, at which inſtant the word is given,

LEFT WING—*March.*

The right wing immediately receives the

CAUTION.

RIGHT-WING,

Halt,

Ready,

Preſent,

Fire,

PRIME-AND-*Load,*

March.

The left-wing marches paſt them till the right-wing being loaded and ſhouldered, receives the word *March.*

LEFT WING,

Halt—Ready, &c.

As directed for the right-wing, and thus they alternately proceed, till each wing has fired twice.

The

The colonel then gives the

CAUTION.

THE LEFT WING WILL FORM LINE ON THE

RIGHT.

RIGHT-WING,

Halt.

When the line is formed,

The colonel gives the

CAUTION,

THE BATTALION WILL ADVANCE,

March.

After marching 50 paces,

Halt.

The colonel gives the

CAUTION.

THE BATTALION WILL FIRE A VOLLEY—FRONT

RANK KNEELING,

MAKE-*Ready*-*Prefent*-*Fire*—PRIME-AND-*Load.*

The colonel gives the

CAUTION;

CAUTION.

THE BATTALION WILL ADVANCE,

March.

When it has advanced 20 paces, it receives the command—

Halt.

And then the

CAUTION.

THE BATTALION WILL FIRE A VOLLEY AND PORT

ARMS.

When the battalion has fired and ported arms,

March.

Dressing by the centre—

Halt.

The front rank comes to the charge—

QUICK—*March.*

The line marches firm and quick, but it is on no account to run. When advanced 50 paces, it receives the word

Halt. They

They come inftantly to the recover and half-cock, and then receive the words

PRIME-AND-*Load*.

The various movements of the light-infantry are defcribed at the beginning of this manœuvre. At the conclufion they affemble in company, and fall in on the left of the battalion.

The battalion is now advanced near the general, in line, with its centre oppofite him.

SEVENTEENTH MANŒUVRE.

RETIRING IN LINE.

RETIRE in line 100 paces.
Retire by alternate half-battalions.
Fire four times.
Retire in line 100 paces or more. *Halt-Front*.

The whole battalion being affembled, the alternate half-battalions fire, the two front ranks ftanding.

The colonel gives the

CAUTION.

THE BATTALION WILL RETIRE,

RIGHT FACE—*March*.

The colonel, while the battalion is retiring, gives the caution that it will fire twice by wings in the retreat, and when it has marched 100 paces, he inftantly gives the   CAUTION,

Caution.

Right-wing, Halt—*Front.*

And when the left one has gained 15 paces, and receives the words *Halt-Front,* the right-wing is inftantly ordered to *Fire,* to *Load,* to *Face* about, and *march* 15 paces beyond the left, where it receives the word *Halt-Front,* on which the left-wing gets that of *Fire,* and in the fame manner alternately proceeds, every due difpatch being made in re-loading.

When the wings have each fired twice,

The colonel gives the

Caution.

The Left-wing will form Line on the Right-wing.

March—Halt.

The battalion is then faced to the right-about, marched 100 paces, *halts* and *fronts.*

In retiring by alternate wings, one colour remains on the inward flank of each half-battalion, to which the men continue to look, by which they move, and before which a directing ferjeant advances 6 paces.

The make ready, prefent, fire, of the advanced wing, is inftantly to fucceed the march of the other advancing wing, or the halt, front, of the retiring.

In the half-battalion firing, advancing, and retreating; if formed two deep, both ranks will fire ftanding; if formed three deep, the front and centre rank
fire

fire standing, and the rear rank remains shouldered in reserve.

Eighteenth Manoeuvre.

Advancing in Line.

ADVANCE in line 100 paces, Halt.
Fire twice, oblique to right and left.
Advance in line 100 paces, Halt.
Fire two volleys. Port arms at the last one, and half-cock.
Open ranks. Advance within 50 paces. Halt, general salute.

In the obliquing, and in the volleys, the front rank kneels.

The music will play, when advancing at open ranks.

The battalion receives the caution to *advance in line*, after marching in ordinary time 100 paces, it is *halted*, and cautioned to *fire a volley obliquely to the right*, and afterwards another *obliquely to the left*, the front rank kneeling.

The battalion advances the same distance, halts, and fires two volleys to the front; after the last, the men Port-*Arms*, Half-*Cock*, Shoulder-*Arms*, and Shut-*pans*.

The *rear ranks* receive the words of command to
TAKE

TAKE OPEN ORDER—QUICK-*march*, the officers come into the front.

The battalion is then cautioned to *Advance*—on the word *March*, the music plays. After marching 50 paces, the line is *halted, arms presented,* colonel and lieutenant-colonel on foot, officers salute, music plays *God save the King,* and drummers beat a march.

The commanding officer then orders, SHOULDER-*Arms,* REAR-*Ranks, take close Order, March.*

END OF THE REVIEW.

MILITARY FUNERALS.

The Maxim at Interments a la Militaire is, that every thing be reversed as far as possible.

THE following form of a colonel's funeral may serve as a model for all others, making allowance for the rank of the deceased.

The party with arms who are to fire over the deceased, form three deep in open ranks, with shouldered arms, and bayonets unfixed, opposite to the place where the corpse lies: on its being brought forth, the officer commanding the party gives the following words of command, *present arms, reverse arms, rear ranks take close order, march. By divisions on the left backward wheel, march, halt, dress.* The officer commanding, places himself with the *rear* division,

and

and the youngest *with that in front*. The serjeants reverse their pikes. The officers hold the points of their swords downwards. On the word *march*, the whole step off in ordinary time.

The Procession in the following Order.

Firing party in sub-divisions.
Drummers, fifers and band of music, beating and playing a dead march:
Chaplain.
The Corpse.

The pall borne by six officers of the same rank as the deceased, in full uniform, black crapes round the left arms and hilts of their swords, white gloves, scarves, and hat bands. The sword of the deceased drawn, and placed across the coffin, on which is likewise placed the sash and gorget.

Privates.
Corporals.
Serjeants.
Staff-officers.
Ensigns.
Lieutenants.
Captains.
Major.
Lieutenant-colonel.
Colonel.

The

The staff-officers, subalterns, and captains, walk two and two, all the officers in their full uniform, crapes round their left arms and hilts of their swords. The non-commission officers and privates with their side-arms only. Drums, fifes, and musical instruments covered with crape.*

On arriving at the burying-ground, the officer of the firing party gives these words of command, *halt, by sub-divisions on the right and left backwards wheel, march. Halt, on reversed arms, rest.*

The corpse and followers pass on, the party is then ordered to *shoulder arms, present arms, shoulder arms, to the right and left wheel and form divisions, march, halt.* On the word march, the party moves on in ordinary time, without music, till it comes to the grave, where the officer orders it *to the right wheel and form line, halt, rear ranks take open order, march.*

The burial service is then performed, † and on its being finished, a signal is given by the commanding officer of the regiment to the officer of the party, who makes it *prime and load, make ready, present, fire*: after firing three times, he orders, *half cock, shoulder arms, shut pans, order arms, fix bayonets, shoulder arms, rear ranks take close order, march; by sub-divisions on the left backward wheel, march, halt, dress.* The officer commanding

---

* *Funerals of Volunteers are also attended by relations.*

† *In Scots regiments, no such ceremony is performed, the signal for firing is the corpse deposited.*

commanding, puts himself at the head of the party, and orders it to march in *quick time*, music playing and drums beating.

On arriving at the regimental parade, the party is dismissed, as all guards are.

The following have been fixed as firing parties for every rank, from a field marshal to a private soldier.

A field-marshal's funeral to be attended by six battalions of infantry, and eight squadrons of cavalry. Three rounds of 15 pieces of cannon over the grave.

A general, four battalions and six squadrons. Three rounds of 11 pieces of cannon.

A lieutenant-general, three battalions and four squadrons. Three rounds of nine pieces of cannon.

A major-general, two battalions and three squadrons. Three rounds of 7 pieces of cannon.

A brigadier-general, one battalion and two squadrons. Three rounds of five pieces of cannon.

A colonel, by his own regiment, or an equal number by detachment, and three rounds of small arms.

A lieutenant-colonel, by 300 men, and three rounds of small arms.

A major, by 200 men, and three rounds of small arms.

A captain by his company, with three rounds of small arms.

A lieutenant, by a lieutenant and 36 men, and three rounds of small arms.

An ensign, by an ensign and 27 men, and three rounds of small arms.

M   Adjutant,

(134)

Adjutant, furgeon, and quarter-mafter, the fame party as an enfign.

A ferjeant, by a ferjeant and 18 men, and three rounds.

A corporal, mufician, drummer, fifer, or privrte, by a ferjeant and 12 men, with three rounds.

A non-commiffioned officer's or private's burial to be attended by the men of the company.

FEU-DE-JOIE; or, REJOICING FIRE,

Is done either by *files*, or by *volley*.—if *by files*, when the word of command is given, the fire begins on the right. each file firing feparately, but as quick after each other as poffible, from right to left; the men are to prefent their pieces high in the air.

It is now more frequently the practice to fire by *vollies*, the whole make ready together, prefenting their pieces in the air. No longer time is allowed between the fires than what is fufficient for the men to load and fhoulder. The ufual time for thefe fires is at one o'clock in the afternoon.

The huzzas after each fire are generally omitted.

FINIS.